Mahāmudrā

H. E. the Twelfth Zurmang Gharwang Rinpoche

MAHĀMUDRĀ

A PRACTICAL GUIDE

His Eminence the Twelfth
Zurmang Gharwang Rinpoche

Foreword by His Holiness the Sakya Trichen

Wisdom

Wisdom Publications
199 Elm Street
Somerville, MA 02144 USA
wisdomexperience.org

Library of Congress Cataloging-in-Publication Data is available.
LCCN 2020051302

ISBN 978-1-61429-587-7 ebook ISBN 978-1-61429-610-2

25 24 23 22 21
5 4 3 2 1

Cover design by Gopa & Ted 2. Interior design by Tony Lulek. Set in Diacritical Garamond Pro 11.9/15.54.

Wisdom Publications' books are printed on acid-free paper and meet the guidelines for permanence and durability of the Production Guidelines for Book Longevity of the Council on Library Resources.

Printed in Canada.

CONTENTS

His Holiness
The Gongma Trichen

Supreme Head of the Sakyapa Order
of Tibetan Buddhism

Foreword

I am very pleased by the publication of this invaluable work. *Mahāmudrā: A Practical Guide* is the twelfth Zurmang Gharwang Rinpoche's translations and commentary on a text written by Bokar Rinpoche, which is itself a concise commentary on the ninth Gyalwa Karmapa Wangchuk Dorjé's *Ocean of Definitive Meaning.*

The latter is one of the most profound texts ever composed on the path of mahāmudrā, and it is used by a number of yogis as a core text in their practice. It is designed to help all serious students of Vajrayāna pursue in earnest their aspiration to attain enlightenment for the sake of all beings.

Gharwang Rinpoche's work serves as a definitive manual, guiding aspiring mahāmudrā students along the complete path, beginning with a clear presentation of the preliminaries, through a detailed presentation of śamatha and vipaśyanā, and concluding with enlightening instructions on the actualization of the result.

I wholeheartedly recommend its dedicated study to all who wish to deepen their understanding of mahāmudrā, and I pray that it may bring countless beings to ultimate realization.

The Sakya Trichen **July 28, 2020**

Dolma Phodrang

192 Rajpur Road, P.O. Box Rajpur, 248009 Dehradun, U.K. India
+91-135-2734081 · sakyadolmaphodrang@gmail.com

PREFACE

THE ZURMANG KAGYU TRADITION has its own unique and profound teachings on mahāmudrā, which are encapsulated in instructions that have been passed down from master to student for over six hundred years. Over the past couple of decades, I have been preparing many students to receive these extraordinary teachings and practices by guiding them in the practice of the Zurmang Kagyu preliminary practices and giving teachings on the Four Thoughts That Turn the Mind toward Dharma and many other foundational topics. Before students progress to the Zurmang Kagyu mahāmudrā practices, I believe it is helpful to first introduce students to the practice of mahāmudrā by way of a concise text that teaches the essentials of mahāmudrā practice. For this purpose, I chose to provide teachings on *A Concise Commentary on the Ocean of Definitive Meaning*, by Bokar Rinpoche (1940–2004), which I received the transmission for from H.E. Gyaltsab Rinpoche.

Bokar Rinpoche was well known as an accomplished meditator in the Karma Kagyu tradition. As the name of his text suggests, *A Concise Commentary on the Ocean of Definitive Meaning* is a commentary of another text called *The Ocean of Definitive Meaning. The Ocean of Definitive Meaning* was written by the ninth Gyalwa Karmapa, Wangchuk Dorjé (1556–1603), and is one of the most profound texts ever written on the practice of mahāmudrā. One could spend an entire lifetime practicing the instructions found within this work. Even today, many yogis in Tibet, India, and Nepal still use this text as the main source for their mahāmudrā practice. It is perhaps best to think of Bokar Rinpoche's text as a distillation of Wangchuk Dorjé's *Ocean of Definitive Meaning*. The text is written in verse, which makes it suitable for memorizing, and it is also written in a way that allows for one to engage in the practices while the verses are recited. These features have made it a popular text to take into retreat. And for these same reasons, I consider it an excellent text for guiding one's daily meditation practice. For instance, with the instruction of a qualified teacher, you can choose a verse and use it to direct your practice for the week, and then the following week you might move on to the next verse, and so on. In this way the text can guide you through a broad range of mahāmudrā instructions, all the way from the preliminary topics on up to profound meditation instructions. The book is structured in such a way that the verses from the root text are in bold, and underneath in plain text is my commentary. Following the commentary is the complete root text in both Tibetan and English translation.

I feel it is important to emphasize that these teachings are meant for serious students of Vajrayāna who have completed the preliminary practices (*ngöndro*), who have faith, perseverance, and unshakable devotion, who engage tirelessly in the path to achieve enlightenment not only for themselves but for all others, and who on top of all this understand the significance of the mahāmudrā teachings, which are profound and vast. If you really wish to practice, then please find a qualified guru who can guide you to train correctly. As with the eighty-four thousand different teachings of the Buddha, the purpose of practicing the instructions found in this text is to leave behind forever the destructive patterns of ego-clinging. It is my hope that through your earnest practice, you will one day reach the same realization as the great gurus of the past.

The twelfth Zurmang Gharwang Rinpoche

INTRODUCTION

Saṃsāra, Nirvāṇa, the Mind, and Buddha Nature

The line between saṃsāra and nirvāṇa is very thin. This is because saṃsāra is simply the projection of our minds, a projection created by confusion. Nirvāṇa is simply freedom from this confusion. You can sit on either side of the line between saṃsāra and nirvāṇa. It's up to you. But although the line is very thin, it takes extraordinary skill and profound wisdom to traverse the path from one side to the other—to dissolve the division itself. This book and these teachings are intended to serve as support for that journey. However, efficient progress along this path requires the guidance of an experienced mahāmudrā master and immense effort on the part of the practitioner.

To be an ordinary sentient being is to fail to recognize your own buddha nature. The moment you recognize your buddha nature, you are awake, and this is what we call "buddhahood," which is also known as "awakening" or "enlightenment." Buddha nature is not something that you have to somehow create. It is already there waiting to be discovered. Imagine a poor person who does not know that in their backyard is a buried treasure. The moment this person finds the treasure, then they are totally free from poverty. Similarly, as long as we fail to recognize the buddha nature that we naturally possess, we will continue to circle in saṃsāra, but the moment we really recognize our buddha nature, we are freed from the darkness of unknowing, and in that moment, we are a buddha. Mahāmudrā practice is the discovery of this treasure of the mind called "buddha nature."

Through the proper guidance of qualified teachers and by making genuine effort we are able to eradicate all forms of obscurations to the revealing of our own buddha nature. We can call it "buddha nature," or the "buddha essence," or, in Sanskrit, *sugatagarbha*, but all these words actually refer to the same thing, the nature of the mind. And this is not something that only humans have. Every being has buddha nature. However, we are very fortunate because we have been born as human beings, which means that we have access to these teachings and have the capacity to put them into practice and become enlightened.

The Nature of the Mind

We might then wonder, what is the mind? What is consciousness, or awareness? In some ways, the mind may seem unreal. It is not something tangible that we could bump into. The mind is not composed of the physical elements of earth, water, fire, or wind. But if the mind is not real in a tangible manner, then how is it that we are able to think and feel and do all the things that we do each day? In Buddhist texts, the reflection of the moon on a lake is used as a metaphor to explain how things do not exist in the way that they appear to us. While they appear to be fully real, substantially existent, and to possess some intrinsic nature of their own, they do not in fact exist in that way. This analogy can help us begin to understand the way that the mind exists.

The essence of the mind is empty. We cannot see the mind, we cannot touch the mind, and in some way, we can say that this essence of the mind is indescribable. But to say that the mind is empty does not mean that the mind is vacuous like space. It is not empty like a void or a vacant room. It is also not devoid of characteristics. Your mind is aware. It has the quality of knowing. The nature of mind is luminosity, which allows for the dawning of appearances. These appearances can come in a variety of forms. Certain forms are consistent with the experience of saṃsāra and certain forms are consistent with the experience of nirvāṇa. Everything that we could experience in saṃsāra or nirvāṇa is a creation of the mind. And all the appearances of the mind are spontaneous. In this way the mind is also described as spontaneous.

Understanding these qualities of the mind—its essence, nature, and characteristics—is fundamental to the features of mahāmudrā practice. For example, in mahāmudrā practice, you may encounter the instruction to not abandon thoughts. This might sound very strange to meditators from other traditions, but if you really understand the nature of the mind, then you will understand the profundity of this instruction. Thoughts are not harmful things in and of themselves. The final goal of mahāmudrā practice is not the cessation of all thoughts. This is not something that we strive for. It is said in the mahāmudrā tradition the essence of thought is the *dharmakāya*, the truth body of a buddha. So, in a certain sense, practicing with the aim to abandon thought would be like aiming to abandon the dharmakāya. In fact, many mahāmudrā masters say that when thoughts arise, they feel so happy and joyful because, for them, more thoughts means more opportunity to experience the dharmakāya.

With this practice, you are encouraged to investigate your thoughts. The idea is that by rubbing the two sticks of thought together—using thought to look at thought—the fire of insight will ignite seemingly from nowhere. Insight does not, of course, actually arise from nowhere. Just as with fuel and fire, there is an intimate connection between thoughts and the dharmakāya, which makes it possible to find the dharmakāya present within thoughts, using the help of the tools of mindfulness and awareness.

Meditation Advice

Meditation has become very popular these days, and this should not be surprising, since a regular meditation practice can be very helpful in taking the edge off the stresses of everyday life. However, the true purpose of Buddhist meditation is to resolve the confusion that is the source of saṃsāra and connect us with an experience that is permeated by a natural, unchanging, and genuine happiness. In Buddhism, meditation is a practice not simply to alleviate stress, but to free you from suffering entirely. This is the ultimate benefit of meditation.

There are two tools of the mind that are crucial for improving the stability and clarity of your meditation practice: mindfulness and awareness. Mindfulness is the activity of the mind that keeps you on task and helps you maintain the continuity for your focus. Awareness monitors the quality of your meditation. Awareness is like a guard who notices if an intruder has entered the space of your meditation; it monitors to see if agitation or dullness are present. These mental tools will equip you with the capacity to tame your wild mind.

One of the specific meditation instructions in the mahāmudrā tradition is to meditate in many shorter meditation sessions rather than one long session. An exhausted mind is not conducive to any type of meditation, but mahāmudrā meditation in particular requires that our minds be fresh and free from dullness. Practicing in shorter sessions also helps us to stay motivated and enthusiastic, so that we can wake up each day looking forward to our meditation practice.

The mind can be very delicate and so we need to be skillful in our approach to training it. For example, if you have a pet who you always keep in a cage, they will always try to run away, and it will be very difficult to get them back in the cage. But if you allow your pet to roam freely and feed them appropriately, then they will automatically always want to stay around you. The mind is similar in that if you try to keep it rigidly locked in the cage of meditation for too long, then the mind will resist meditating.

It is also important to sit in a comfortable position while meditating. When practicing meditation, we are usually directed to close the eyes, or partially close the eyes, but when practicing mahāmudrā meditation, it is advised to keep your eyes completely open. Then, sitting comfortably, simply allow thoughts to arise and cease. You don't have to do anything for this to occur. It is a thought's nature to arise and cease by itself. During meditation, don't think about the past. The past is like fishing from an empty riverbed. The past no longer exists, so fixating on it will likely only make you sad or agitated. Don't fall into the trap of imagining the future either. This is like trying to paint the face of an unborn child. It is impossible to know something that has yet to exist, so getting lost in daydreams about the future is a pointless exercise. Our focus should instead be on the present, on this very moment. Ultimately, you will discover the present moment is also something that you cannot hold on to, just like writing in water. It is difficult to find and beyond expression.

It is important that you come to some determination about the mind based on your own experience. You cannot simply rest on the knowledge of what your teacher said or what a text says. Instead, you must look for yourself and see what you discover. This does not mean that you shouldn't follow the guidance of an experienced meditation teacher. These meditation advices are like a technology that you can use to discover the nature of your mind.

When you meditate, it is important to relax as you watch your thoughts arise, abide, and cease. If you get carried away by your thoughts, then as soon as you notice that you are distracted, gently come back to the awareness observing the thoughts. You can also begin to introspect, to inquire: What is the mind? Is it the same as the thoughts? Is it different from the thoughts? Where is the mind? Is it outside of the body? Is it inside of the body? If it is inside your body, then in which part of your body does it reside? What is the shape of this mind? What color is the mind? Is it blue, green, yellow, or red? Through your own experience, you need to come to the determination yourself of the impossibility of the mind having a shape, a color, etc. If you determine that the mind is empty, inquire into what that actually means. For instance, is the emptiness of the mind like the empty space in your room? Or is it a different kind of emptiness? And if you determine that the mind is luminous, then inquire into what the luminosity is. Is the luminosity of the mind something like a light? Something like the brightness of the sun? Keep exploring deeper into the nature of your mind. Then you will come to know the nature of the mind through experience. It may take some time, but persist in looking at the mind, investigating in such a manner.

Once you know the essence of mind, then you will realize that it is not expressible in words, because words only capture and convey ordinary conceptual thought, but the essence of mind goes beyond ordinary expression and even beyond ordinary thinking. Even the omniscient Buddha who could explain everything often kept silent when it came to discussions of emptiness or the essence of the mind. According to many teachers, silence is often the best answer, because the very act of trying to express the ultimate in words is in some ways misleading.

In this book, the main verses, in bold, are excellent prompts for your meditation practice. You could work through this text, taking a verse or two as your meditation prompt for a week, and then moving on to the next verse the following week. It may be helpful to break your daily meditation session into a number of shorter periods of five to ten minutes with short breaks in between. In this way, you can keep your meditation on the verses inspired and avoid drifting into daydreaming or dullness. If you make effort using this method, you will certainly see progress. Of course, as you become more adept, you will eventually be able to extend the duration of the sessions while keeping your meditation fresh. You should experiment and learn for yourself the ideal session length during which you are able to maintain the quality of your meditation.

The Difference between Realization and Experience

In the mahāmudrā tradition we make a distinction between understanding, experience, and realization. First, when we receive teachings, whether it is a basic or more profound teaching, we are developing a type of understanding of the topic at hand. As we listen and start to develop an understanding of the subject, we may even gain some type of experience. Imagine that you had never tasted chocolate before, and someone begins to explain to you what it is like to taste chocolate. First, you learn that chocolate is sweet, and then you might even start to imagine the experience of the taste of chocolate. However, we should not confuse the understanding of the thing and the imaginative experience of that thing with the actual experience of it. When you are learning something new, you will gradually develop a general concept of the subject. For example, when you begin to learn about emptiness, through many different lines of reasoning you will arrive at an understanding of emptiness. In Tibetan, this kind of understanding is called *gowa* (*go ba*). As you contemplate the subject and refine your understanding, you may gain a little experience, and think, "Aha, that is what emptiness must be like." This type of experience is called *nyam nyong* (*nyams myong*) in Tibetan. However, this experience still does not qualify as realization. Realization requires that we completely and directly realize the nature of a particular thing without any illusion, and without any mistake. This is realization, which is called *tokpa* (*rtogs pa*) in Tibetan. While it is my sincere hope that this book will be helpful, it will only be of limited use unless you support your learning with practice, and your practice will only really be effective if it is guided by a realized master.

As your practice deepens, you will encounter a variety of experiences. These might be waves of great bliss or deep sadness. Know that this is part and parcel of progress on the path. It happens to everyone. When these types of experience arise, it is important not to fixate on them or ruminate over them, but to simply let them be. Many practitioners have come to me and said, "Oh, Rinpoche, I had this amazing experience when I was in meditation, but now it is gone. How can I get it back?" These types of experiences should not be the goal of your meditation practice. The fact that these experiences are not stable is a sign that they are not genuine realizations. Experiences are like mist—they slowly fade away. It is important to know that chasing these experiences does not lead to realization and actually creates obstacles. And even if you are able to achieve these states from time to time, this can be like building a golden prison, because progress on the path requires you to abandon all forms of attachment, even attachment to pleasurable meditative experiences. When you do not concern yourself with different levels of experience and simply persist with meditation, then this will eventually lead to realization.

You may know this common metaphor for the practice of meditation: when you stir up a lake, the water gets very cloudy, but once the water is allowed to settle, you will be able to clearly see the bottom once again. Similarly, if you allow these experiences to simply be and at the same time watch the mind directly, then your meditation practice will gradually become more lucid, profound, and stable, and this will lead to realization.

The moment you attain realizations on the path, many forms of obscurations, especially the coarse obscurations, will immediately be eradicated, just as when you enter a dark room and flick on the light switch, the darkness instantly disappears. It does not matter if the room had been dark for a thousand years. It will instantly go away. It is like this with realization and obscuration. Of course, until you reach buddhahood, subtle forms of obscurations will remain.

The Meaning of Mahāmudrā

There are many ways of explaining the meaning of mahāmudrā. Dakpo Rinpoche (Gampopa) explained mahāmudrā by referring to the three words that make up the Tibetan translation of mahāmudrā: *chak gya chenpo* (*phyag rgya chen po*). Gampopa explained that *chak*, which literally means "hand," refers to the realization that all appearances, whether they be the appearances of saṃsāra or nirvāṇa, are similar in that they never transcend the dharmatā, that which is unarisen. This is incredibly profound. The next word, *gya,* which literally means "seal," refers to the existence of all these appearances, which remains within the natural state, the ultimate truth. When you realize that all of this is self-liberated, this is the meaning of *chenpo,* which literally means "great." Mahāmudrā has the meaning that appearances do not transcend the dharmatā, which is unarisen, that all of existence falls within the truth of the natural state, and that the realization of this is self-liberating.

We can also explain mahāmudrā in terms of the ground, path, and result: (1) the mahāmudrā of the all-pervasive ground (*gzhi kun la khyab pa'i phyag rgya chen po*), (2) the mahāmudrā of the practice of the path (*lam nyams su len pa'i phyag rgya chen po*), and (3) the mahāmudrā of the spontaneously accomplished result (*'bras bu lhun gyi grub pa'i phyag rgya chen po*).

As for the mahāmudrā of the ground, in many sūtras and tantras, it is stated that all beings possess buddha nature, and that this is the essence of the mind, which is luminous and empty. This is the dharmatā of the foundation of all, which is called the mahāmudrā of the ground. By practicing the mahāmudrā of the path, one realizes buddha nature through understanding the freedom from fabrication and emptiness, which reveals that all phenomena are selfless. Finally, whenever the four kāyas and the five wisdoms of the Buddha are acquired, this is called the mahāmudrā of the result.

We can also understand mahāmudrā by way of its five unique characteristics: (1) In terms of the view, the right view does not depend on either scripture or reasoning; the perfect realization of the view actually dawns within. (2) In terms of meditation, dullness and agitation dissolve in their own place without requiring effort in concentration, like snow dissolving upon falling on a hot surface. (3) In terms of samaya, mahāmudrā relies on uncontaminated samaya, which is continuously present and does not require guarding. (4) In terms of conduct, normally we must rely on applying the right antidote, but in mahāmudrā, the practices of adopting what is beneficial and discarding what is harmful is like a knot that naturally unties itself. (5) In terms of the result, without relying on any sign, the result is already spontaneously present and self-arisen.

Now, let us turn to the text to unravel some of these descriptions of mahāmudrā.

A CONCISE COMMENTARY ON

THE OCEAN OF DEFINITIVE MEANING

Easy-to-Implement Root Verses for Unlocking the Door to the Definitive Meaning

ཕྱག་ཆེན་ངེས་དོན་རྒྱ་མཚོའི་བསྡུས་དོན་རྩ་ཚིག་ཁྱེར་བདེར་བཀོད་པ་ངེས་དོན་
སྒོ་འབྱེད་ཅེས་བྱ་བ་བཞུགས་སོ།།

Root Verses by Ven. Bokar Rinpoche

Translation and Commentary by His Eminence
the Twelfth Zurmang Gharwang Rinpoche

THE TITLE AND OPENING VERSE

The complete title of Bokar Rinpoche's text is *A Concise Commentary on the Ocean of Definitive Meaning: Easy-to-Implement Root Verses for Unlocking the Door to the Definitive Meaning.* As discussed in the introduction, this work is a distillation of the important points from one of the most profound texts on mahāmudrā: *The Ocean of Definitive Meaning*, by the ninth Karmapa, Wangchuk Dorjé.

According to the traditional protocol for composing a treatise, the text begins with a verse of prostration and going for refuge:

The guru, the deity, and one's own mind,
being indivisible, are one in the natural state,
to which I prostrate and
wholeheartedly go for refuge at all times.

In general, the Buddhist object of refuge is the triple gem, the Buddha, Dharma, and Sangha, but in Vajrayāna Buddhism, we also take refuge in the three roots: the guru who is the root of blessings, the deity who is the root of accomplishment, and the dharma protectors and ḍākinīs who are the root of activities. Here, instead of the dharma protectors and ḍākinīs, we have one's own mind. This signifies that although relatively speaking we may see many different forms, in terms of the ultimate truth, the guru, the yidams, and our mind are all inseparable. This verse honors this truth.

Bokar Rinpoche has kindly arranged this text for those who are interested in making a closer connection with the mahāmudrā instructions. He composed this text in such a way that it contains all of the essential points, but at the same time it is also concise and practically suitable for guiding one's meditation practice. There are three main sections of the text: (1) preliminaries, (2) actual practice, and (3) conclusion. We will now turn to the section on preliminaries.

PART I: THE PRELIMINARIES

IN ORDER TO PRACTICE mahāmudrā meditation effectively, it is essential that you first prepare your mind. The great yogis of the past have developed a set of trainings called the preliminary practices, which help us to generate the right motivation, set our minds in a good place, clear away karmic obstacles, and generate positive energy. Engaging in these preliminary practices readies the mind for mahāmudrā meditation.

To dive straight into mahāmudrā practice without first engaging in these preliminary practices is like heading off on a journey into unknown territory without a map. Who knows where you will end up? Thus, perhaps somewhat counterintuitively, it does not save you time to skip these practices; by skipping these practices you will most likely end up only wasting your time.

This text outlines and gives advice on three different sets of preliminary practices: (1) the common preliminaries, (2) the uncommon preliminaries, and (3) the special preliminaries. We will begin with the common preliminaries.

1. THE COMMON PRELIMINARIES

THROUGH PRACTICING the common preliminaries, you develop the motivation to focus your time and energy on meaningful endeavors. These preliminaries are a set of contemplations that help you transform the way you engage with and experience the world. They are called "common" because they are based on ideas that are shared with all Buddhist traditions.

The common preliminaries consist of contemplating and meditating on four different topics: (1) the difficulty of acquiring this life with its opportunities and resources, (2) death and impermanence, (3) karmic cause and effect, and (4) the faults of saṃsāra.

The Difficulty of Acquiring This Life with Its Opportunities and Resources

Namo gurubhyaḥ

In order to practice the excellent Dharma correctly, one must abandon wandering.

The first object of meditation is the fact that this excellent foundation,

which is endowed with the eight opportunities and ten resources,
is difficult to acquire, and since it is extremely beneficial,
it is just like a wish-fulfilling jewel.

The world is full of distractions. There are endless calls for our attention. As the verse states, if you wish to practice Dharma correctly, then you must give up wandering, allowing your precious time to be led and dictated by distractions. We must remain mindful to prevent our life from being guided by the pushes and pulls of mundane life. If we are not careful, all the various endeavors of worldly life will distract us from our Dharma practice.

One of the first points that a Buddhist practitioner is guided to contemplate is how fortunate they are. I know that life is not always easy, and it is certainly never perfect. Indeed, the focus of subsequent contemplations will include the hardships of life. But at this point, we are bringing to mind all the excellent conditions that we are fortunate to have in our lives. When you spend the time to meditate on the things you can be thankful for in your life, then you begin to appreciate that your life is truly a precious opportunity. This insight provides the motivation to use your opportunity wisely and to ensure that you are spending your time on the most meaningful endeavors. In short, the goal of this contemplation is to spark within you the inspiration to practice Dharma.

The verse above presents the traditional way of going about this contemplation, which is to reflect on your human life as an excellent basis for practicing Dharma since it is endowed with eight opportunities and ten resources. This list of opportunities and resources is a technical way of talking about the opportunity that this life affords us.

In Buddhist texts, we are advised to reflect on the fact that, as human beings, we have eight kinds of opportunities, or eight kinds of freedom, because we are free from rebirth in eight states in which one is unable to practice the Dharma:

1. in the hell realm
2. in the hungry ghost realm
3. in the animal realm
4. in the god realm
5. in a barbarian land
6. with incomplete sense faculties
7. in a place where wrong views prevail
8. at a time when a buddha has not come

In addition to being free from these eight kinds of unfortunate rebirths, there are also ten kinds of resources that we have in virtue of being born as a human in this world:

1. We have been born in an era in which a buddha has come.
2. We have been born at a time when a buddha has not only come but has taught the Dharma.
3. The teachings have survived to the present time at which we live.
4. There is a community of people who follow the teachings.
5. There are favorable conditions for practicing Dharma.
6. We have been born as a human being.
7. We have been born in a developed society.
8. Our faculties are intact.
9. We are able to make a living practicing right livelihood.
10. We have faith in the three collections, or the *tripiṭaka*, of Buddha's teachings.

The eight kinds of opportunities as well as ten kinds of resources are very difficult to acquire, and are like a great, beneficial gift.

Sometimes the Buddhist texts can be very technical, but here the essence of the contemplation is to reflect on all the forms of freedom, opportunities, and resources that you enjoy in your life. You are so fortunate to have this life. What will you do with it? How will you choose to spend your precious time?

In particular, by relying on Vajrayāna,
this vajra body, which is endowed with the six elements
for attaining enlightenment in a single lifetime, is even
more rare.

This text is aimed at guiding Vajrayāna practitioners in particular, and in the tantric texts of Mantrayāna it is explained that we all have a vajra body, which is a spiritual body that is subtler than our physical bodies. These texts explain that we are fortunate not only because we have this precious human rebirth, but also because we have this vajra body, which is considered even rarer and more precious than the physical human body. This is because the vajra body possesses the six elements, which enable the attainment of enlightenment within a single lifetime. These six elements are the four of earth, water, fire, and air, together with space and consciousness. In the technology of the Vajrayāna system, these elements of our subtle body are utilized in visualization and yogic practices that provide a quick and powerful path to awakening.

We are incredibly fortunate to have encountered the Vajrayāna teachings. The Buddha said that there may be no tantric teachings for many eons at a time, so having the opportunity to listen to and practice the Vajrayāna teachings is extremely rare and precious.

Moreover, [this precious human rebirth] is difficult to
acquire
in virtue of the three of cause, example, and number,
and even if it is acquired, it is extremely easy to die.
Thus, from now on, one should strive at meditating on the
genuine, excellent Dharma.

Here we are given these strategies for contemplating the rarity and difficulty of acquiring a precious human rebirth: the causes, an example, and the number.

The first strategy is the causes. It is said that there are many different types of rebirth and that to be born a human being with all the freedoms and resources to practice Dharma is extremely rare and difficult because it requires the accumulation of an enormous amount of positive karma in previous lives. It is quite amazing to be reborn as a human if you think about the vast amount of merit that is required for such a life. Moreover, in most of one's previous births one is likely to have been occupied with striving for relief from pain, escaping danger, or absorbed by the intoxication of the god realms, all of which make efforts at accumulating positive karma almost impossible.

"The example" refers to a famous story in the Buddhist texts that describes how rare it is to be born human. A blind turtle lives deep in the ocean, and every hundred years or so, the turtle rises to the ocean's surface to take a breath. On this vast ocean floats a small golden yoke. Now, consider what might be the chances for the turtle to rise up and poke his head through that golden yoke? It is said that the chances of attaining a human rebirth are about the same as the blind turtle rising up and poking his head through the golden yoke. Contemplating the difficulty of acquiring a human rebirth in terms of this example, or metaphor, is the second strategy for meditating on the rarity and difficulty of acquiring a precious human rebirth.

The third strategy is to contemplate how the number of sentient beings—even just those we can see on this planet—is incredibly large, and the proportion of living creatures that are human is incredibly small. Considering these numbers alone, the odds of obtaining a precious human body with these eight opportunities and ten resources are extremely low. This is contemplating in terms of number.

Not only is a human rebirth incredibly rare and difficult to obtain, but even if it is obtained, life is extremely delicate; it does not take much to die. Therefore, we should think, "From now on, I will strive at practicing the pure Dharma."

Death and Impermanence

Having reflected upon our opportunities and resources and understanding how rare and precious our lives are, we then move on to the second of the common preliminaries, which is meditating on impermanence and death.

> **All conditioned phenomena—external and internal, the environment and beings—**
> **are impermanent, even momentarily, in accordance with the four ends.**

If we look at the variety of things and living creatures in the world, one thing we will discover is that they are all impermanent. Look at the things around you: is there anything that will remain forever? What about your home and possessions? What about your thoughts and feelings? What about your family and friends?

In the verse above, "external" refers to all the objects in the world and "internal" refers to the mind. It becomes obvious upon reflection that all these things are impermanent. However, it goes deeper than that. All these things are not only impermanent, but they are also momentary. This means that they are not only impermanent in terms of gross impermanence, like a car that inevitably breaks eventually, but they are changing moment by moment—they do not remain the same even for a second.

The text encourages us to contemplate impermanence in the context of the four extremes. This means we should reflect on these facts: (1) once you are born you have to die, (2) whatever you acquire you will eventually lose, (3) whoever rises to the top will eventually fall, and (4) whoever you meet with, you must ultimately be parted from.

> **In particular, the lifespan of beings is**
> **like a butter lamp in the midst of a windstorm**
> **and like a water bubble.**
> **Indeed, I will certainly die;**
> **the time of death is uncertain, yet death will come soon.**
> **There are many conditions for death,**
> **and though I may not want to, I will die nonetheless.**

There is no one whatsoever who has been able to overcome death.
When I die, I will continuously experience unbearable suffering,
and at that time, there is no refuge apart from the excellent Dharma.
Therefore, I should control my mind, develop disillusionment,
and with a strong sense of urgency, throw myself into the practice of virtue.

Do you know anyone who is immortal? I'm guessing that the answer is no. It is very unlikely that you will be the first exception, the first person to live forever. Dying is part of the natural order of things. Our lives are extremely delicate. The conditions required for life are feeble and there are so many things that can end our lives.

There is something very powerful about combining these two contemplations: reflecting on all the things so wonderful about your life, and then contemplating the impermanence of this precious life. The goal of combining these is to create an orientation to the world in which you are highly motivated to do something meaningful with your precious life and to start now because you understand that this opportunity might not be available for long—it might even be gone tomorrow.

We should recognize that there is no time to lose, and because of this we should develop a feeling of weariness toward useless and meaningless activities. We should recognize the urgency of this situation and develop an attitude that is motivated toward devoting all of our spare time to the practice of what is meaningful and beneficial to ourselves and others. The Buddhist masters say that the possibility of a good death, one that is not plagued by regret, is provided by having lived a good and meaningful life.

Karmic Cause and Effect

Having reflected upon death and impermanence, we next contemplate the forces that determine the experience we will have after we have died. The third contemplation is a meditation on karmic cause and effect.

> **After death, like a butter lamp whose oil is depleted,**
> **I will have no power over where I am born.**
> **Without any control, I will certainly follow my karma.**
> **In general, all the variety of appearances of happiness and suffering**
> **are said to be the results of virtuous and nonvirtuous karma.**
>
> **Moreover, one should contemplate in detail how,**
> **due to engaging in the ten virtues, one will be reborn in the higher realms,**
> **and due to engaging in the ten nonvirtues under the control of mental afflictions,**
> **one will be reborn in the lower realms.**
>
> **In short, the results of my own actions will never disappear,**
> **but I will certainly experience them.**
> **Therefore, I should strive at the proper way of**
> **adopting virtue and discarding vice,**
> **and investigate my own mental continuum.**

During the moments after your death, you will be propelled toward another life by the force of karma. Most people do not have the capacity to intervene in the death process to influence where they will be reborn. The journey after death is not like your last planned vacation. Instead, it is as if you find yourself on a plane heading toward an unknown destination, based on a ticket you accidentally purchased a long time ago. At the time of death, you are forced to follow the results of your karma: whatever physical, verbal, or mental actions you have undertaken in the past. This is because once a cause has been put in place, the result will never simply disappear; instead it must come to fruition at some point in the future. If you cultivate the habit of engaging in acts of virtue, then you will attain the happiness of the three superior rebirths in the human, demigod, and god realms. Alternatively, if you commit actions of nonvirtue, you will be reborn in the three lower realms: the animal realm, the hungry ghost realm, and the hell realm.

So, rather than panicking at the time of death, worrying about what is happening, what will come next, and what you might do about it, it is better to act now by paying close attention to the conduct of your body, speech, and mind as you go through your day. We should make efforts in right conduct, and look inside, contemplate, and analyze to ensure that we are acting in accord with our values.

Faults of Saṃsāra

Having contemplated the fact that all our experiences of happiness and suffering are the result of our past actions of virtue or nonvirtue, we next reflect on the fact that even if we spend our entire life engaged in virtue and are reborn into a life with wonderful conditions, any birth within saṃsāra will always be characterized by suffering and dissatisfaction. So, the final contemplation of the four common preliminaries is meditating on the faults of saṃsāra.

> **Wherever one is born among the six classes of beings**
> **within the three realms of saṃsāra,**
> **One will be thoroughly and continuously**
> **oppressed by the three kinds of suffering.**
> **Moreover, one should contemplate how one will experience**
> **these forms of suffering intensely and for a long time:**
> **the suffering of heat and cold as a hell being,**
> **the suffering of hunger and thirst as a hungry ghost,**

the suffering of eating one another as an animal,
the suffering of birth, old age, sickness, and death, etc., as a human,
the suffering of quarrelling as a demigod,
and the suffering of dying and falling from the status of a god.

In order to understand how even the most excellent lives in saṃsāra can still be considered to be characterized by suffering, we need to understand that the Buddhist concept of suffering does not simply refer to physical pain or mental anguish. Buddhist texts explain three different types of suffering: (1) the suffering of suffering, (2) the suffering of change, and (3) all-pervasive conditioned suffering.

The "suffering of suffering" refers to the unpleasant feelings, such as physical and mental pain. The "suffering of change" is a little counterintuitive, because it actually refers to pleasant feelings. This is because pleasant feelings are not stable and are, in a sense, only the beginning of the dissatisfaction that inevitably follows. Let me give you an example. Imagine that you have been sitting on an airplane for a very long flight and having just landed you are able to stand for the first time in hours. As soon as you stand up, it will feel like such a pleasant relief. Now, imagine that having arrived, you are asked to wait in a long line at customs, there is nowhere to sit, for some reason the line is not moving, and you now have to stand for what seems like hours. The happiness of standing has now changed into the suffering of standing! This is an example of the suffering of change. If the things that give us pleasant feelings truly had the nature of bestowing pleasant feelings, then we could always rely on them as a basis for happiness. Unfortunately, even the pleasant things of saṃsāra cannot be relied upon for genuine and lasting happiness.

The third kind of suffering, all-pervasive conditioned suffering, refers to the five aggregates and their relationship with suffering and saṃsāra. It is because our bodies and minds are under the influence of fundamental ignorance, negative emotions, and past karma that we suffer. The root of saṃsāra is our fundamental ignorance about the true nature of ourselves and the world and about the true causes of happiness and suffering. It is due to that fundamental misunderstanding that we unwittingly and inevitably continue to create the conditions to suffer in the future. Within the three realms, no matter which of the six classes of beings one takes birth as, there is no corner in which we can hide from suffering. For instance, hell beings continually suffer either cold or heat. Those reborn as hungry ghosts always suffer thirst and hunger. Those reborn as animals experience the suffering of being preyed upon. Human beings suffer the experiences of birth, old age, sickness, and death. If you are born as a demigod, you are always fighting. In the higher realms, there is said to be a jambu tree, which is a wish-fulfilling tree that produces delicious fruit. The trunk is in the demigod realm, but the fruit is in the god realm, and so the demigods are never able to enjoy it. They are continually jealous and quarrelling with one another, and never content. The gods are always happy, until it comes time to die, when they have five signs that tell them where they will fall, and they experience extreme torment at being forced to fall from the pleasurable status of a god to a lower rebirth. This story is meant to convey that no matter your conditions, no matter how rich you might be, there is no place in saṃsāra that is free from suffering. The three realms of saṃsāra are like a wheel of suffering, which cycles and repeats again and again, and all are pervaded by suffering.

> **Even the slightest appearance**
> **of pleasure or riches within saṃsāra**
> **should be abandoned like poisoned food.**
> **Now is the time to strive at the method for**
> **definitely liberating oneself from saṃsāra, which is like a fire pit.**

No matter where you go, if you carry your ignorance, desire, and aversion with you, then you are sure to suffer. From this perspective, whatever you see as happiness within saṃsāra is very minor, insignificant, and transient. You should understand that all these pleasures are like poisonous food, which one may enjoy in the moment, but which will soon turn to pain and suffering. Thus, you should reject these superficial pleasures just as you would throw away poisoned food. Saṃsāra is like a fire pit in that there is no genuine relief to be found while within it. Thus, you should contemplate that now is the time to find a method to free yourself from saṃsāra.

2. THE UNCOMMON PRELIMINARIES

While the four *common* preliminaries are found in the teachings of all traditions of Buddhism, the four *uncommon* preliminaries are unique to the Vajrayāna tradition of Buddhism. The four uncommon preliminaries are (1) refuge and prostrations, (2) Vajrasattva meditation and recitation, (3) maṇḍala offering, and (4) guru yoga.

Refuge and Prostrations

Having developed the wish to be free of the three types of suffering that characterize saṃsāra, it is natural to look for a way to free yourself from saṃsāra and its suffering. For a Buddhist, the solution lies in what are called the three jewels: the Buddha, the Dharma, and the Sangha. In this context, the practice of refuge is combined with the practice of visualization and the performance of prostrations.

> **Therefore, apart from the three jewels,**
> **there is no refuge that can protect me from the suffering of existence.**

Thus, I and all beings that fill the expanse of space go for refuge
and visualize as follows:

In the space in front of me is a wish-fulfilling tree with five branches.
In the middle, sitting atop a lion throne, lotus, and moon,
is my root guru, Lord Vajradhāra, clear and brilliant,
and complete with the major and minor marks.

Above that are the lineage gurus in tiers:
in front, on the right, behind, and on the left, respectively,
sit the yidam, the Buddha, the Dharma, and the Sangha,
gathered like a heap of clouds.

I and all beings go for refuge until attaining complete enlightenment,
and develop supreme bodhicitta.
Finally, the objects of refuge melt into light and,
dissolving into my own three doors,
rest in the natural state.

Why do we need to engage in the practice of prostrations? Prostrations not only purify our negative karma, but they also help to transform our minds so that we become a suitable vessel for the Dharma. Prostrations incline us toward the Dharma; they are a practice of humility, and when practiced together with going for refuge and developing bodhicitta, they set our motivation so that whatever we do becomes the cause for liberation.

In preparation for the practice of prostrations, we first visualize the refuge tree as follows: In the space in front of us, there is a beautiful meadow filled with singing birds and beautiful creatures. In the center, there is a splendid lake with the qualities of pure water: crystal clear, cool, sweet, light, soft, soothing to the stomach, free of impurities, and with the quality that clears the throat. In the middle of the lake is a magnificent tree with five branches. In the center, one's root guru sits atop a lion throne, lotus, and moon disk. One's root guru is in the form of Vajradhāra, adorned by the thirty-two major and eighty minor marks of a saṃbhogakāya, or the complete enjoyment body of a buddha. All of the lineage gurus are stacked above the root guru, with Vajradhāra at the top. From Vajradhāra's perspective, in the front are all the yidam deities, on the right side are the buddhas of the ten directions, behind is the Dharma in the form of sacred texts, on the left are the eight bodhisattvas, and surrounding this assembly in the sky are a host of other gurus like a cloud. In front of them, visualize yourself together with all sentient beings going for refuge to the three jewels until enlightenment, and give rise to bodhicitta, the aspiration to attain complete enlightenment for the sake of freeing all sentient beings from the suffering of saṃsāra. Then, all the other gurus dissolve into your root guru, who melts into light and then dissolves into yourself. At this point, rest in the nature of the mind.

Vajrasattva

The second of the uncommon preliminaries is Vajrasattva meditation and recitation. This meditation on Vajrasattva and the recitation of Vajrasattva mantras help to purify your negative karma, harmful habit patterns, and obscurations, like your destructive emotions and ignorance.

> **I confess all negativities and downfalls accumulated from beginningless time**
> **by means of the four powers, and in particular,**
> **I shall engage in the supreme power of applying the antidote,**
> **undertaking the meditation and recitation of Vajrasattva:**
>
> **Myself in ordinary form,**
> **sitting atop my crown is Guru Vajrasattva, body white in color;**

his right hand holds a five-pointed vajra at his heart;
his left hand holds a bell at his hip;
he is seated in the bodhisattva posture.

Appearing, yet essenceless, within his body, at his luminous heart,
atop a moon disk, is a *hūṃ* surrounded by the hundred-syllable mantra.
From that a stream of nectar descends and enters through the aperture of Brahmā,
purifying all of one's negativities, obscurations, and defilements without exception.

Having recited [the mantra] again and again, Vajrasattva becomes pleased,
and grants confirmation with the words
"All your negativities and obscurations are purified!"
He melts into light and dissolves into me,
whereby I become indivisible with the three vajras.

The visualization for the Vajrasattva meditation and recitation is as follows: Visualize yourself in your ordinary form and visualize your root guru in the form of Vajrasattva seated on your crown, white in color, right hand holding a vajra at the heart, left hand holding a bell at the hip, and seated in the full vajra posture. Although the guru appears as Vajrasattva, he is insubstantial like the reflection of the moon in water. In the heart of Vajrasattva is a moon disk, upon which is a white *hūṃ* surrounded by the hundred-syllable mantra revolving clockwise. As you recite the hundred-syllable mantra, nectar flows down from the heart of your guru into your body, entering through your crown, and purifying the all negative actions of body, speech, and mind.

After you have repeated this visualization and recitation a number of times, Vajrasattva becomes very pleased and says, "O son/daughter, all your defilements have become eradicated!" Vajrasattva then dissolves into you, and your body, speech, and mind become indivisible with the completely pure body, speech, and mind of Vajrasattva.

This practice should be done utilizing the four powers. The four powers are the following: (1) The power of the basis involves going for refuge and generating bodhicitta. Since all negative actions are carried out toward either the three jewels or toward sentient beings, refuge and bodhicitta enable us to transform the objects of our past negative actions into the basis for our purification of those actions. This is because going for refuge involves placing our trust in the three jewels and developing bodhicitta is the altruistic attitude seeking to attain enlightenment in order to liberate all sentient beings from the suffering of saṃsāra. (2) The power of regret involves developing remorse for whatever negative actions we have undertaken in the past. (3) The power of resolve involves the commitment to refrain from future wrongdoing. (4) The power of engaging in the antidote involves undertaking some positive activity to counteract the negative deed that one intends to purify. One of the most powerful antidotes is the practice of meditating on Vajrasattva together with reciting Vajrasattva's hundred-syllable mantra.

Maṇḍala Offering

The third of the uncommon preliminaries is the maṇḍala offering. This practice helps one to complete the two accumulations required for awakening: the accumulation of merit and the accumulation of wisdom.

In reliance on the supreme method of offering a pure realm,
one should amass the two collections of merit and wisdom.
Visualize as follows:
The practice maṇḍala is made of precious substances,
unsullied by the stains of faults.

In front of oneself, properly visualize

a luminous celestial mansion, with completely perfect attributes,
in the middle of which are one's root and lineage gurus, surrounded in the four directions
by the yidam, Buddha, Dharma, and Sangha,
together with *vīras*, ḍākinīs, and wisdom protectors.
Visualize a maṇḍala offering adorned with billions [of universes],
including Mount Meru, the four continents, and four subcontinents.

Furthermore, visualize and offer everything that exists without exception—
the bodies, wealth, and collections of virtue,
belonging to oneself and all beings equal to the expanse of space.
By this power, may the two collections be fully completed.
The deities, being delighted, melt into light and dissolve into me,
and we become nondual.

In this practice, you use the power of your imagination to visualize that you are offering a maṇḍala of a pure realm to the merit field. It is best to own two maṇḍalas, one to be kept in front of the altar and one to offer in your practice. When visualizing the maṇḍala, imagine a world that includes Mount Meru in the center surrounded by the four continents and four subcontinents. In front of you is a celestial mansion that includes within it the entire merit field, which includes all objects of refuge: the guru, yidam, Buddha, Dharma, Sangha, surrounded by the vīras, or heroes, and ḍākinīs. Then to these objects of refuge make the offering of a pure realm along with all the wealth, virtues, and good things in the world. Then imagine that the deities are delighted and that they then melt into light and dissolve into you and become inseparable from you. The practice of offering a maṇḍala is a powerful way to accumulate the collections of merit and wisdom.

Guru Yoga

The final of the four uncommon preliminaries is the practice of guru yoga, which enables you to quickly receive blessings.

The foundation of all good qualities,
and particularly the supreme method for realizing the ultimate, mahāmudrā,
is nothing other than the blessing of the glorious guru.

Thus, perform guru yoga as follows:
Visualizing myself as the yidam deity,
on my crown is my root guru, Lord Vajradhāra,
above whom sit the lineage gurus, one atop the other,
and surrounded by yidams, buddhas, bodhisattvas,
vīras, ḍākinīs, and wisdom protectors.

Through the power of making offerings and reciting prayers to them,
the surrounding retinue dissolves into the principal guru.
The principal guru then encompasses the nature of all objects of refuge.
Once more, I request the bestowal of empowerment,
and the four empowerments are received.

The four obscurations are purified, and the seeds for the four kāyas are planted.
Then, the guru, being delighted, melts into light
and dissolves into me,
and I remain in the state of mahāmudrā.

It is said that the guru is the foundation of all knowledge and good qualities, and in particular, whoever wants to achieve the realization of mahāmudrā must rely on the blessings of the guru. First, visualize yourself as the yidam, like Vajrayoginī, since it is said that if you visualize yourself in ordinary form, the blessings cannot enter you. On your crown is the guru in the form of Vajradhāra, and above Vajradhāra are all the lineage gurus. The gurus are encircled by the yidams, ḍākas, ḍākinīs, and protectors. Recite a guru yoga invocation like "Calling the Guru from Afar," etc. Due to these prayers, the lineage gurus dissolve into your root guru, who becomes inseparable from all objects of refuge.

Request empowerment from the guru, and then imagine the guru bestowing the four empowerments, purifying all your defilements: (1) afflictive obscurations, (2) obscurations to knowledge, (3) obscurations to concentration, and (4) obscurations of body, speech, and mind. In addition, the seeds for the four kāyas, or enlightened bodies of a buddha, are planted: (1) nirmāṇakāya, the emanation body, (2) saṃbhogakāya, the complete enjoyment body, (3) the jñānadharmakāya, the wisdom truth body, and (4) the svabhāvakāya, the nature body. The guru becomes exceedingly pleased, melts into light, and dissolves into you. Your body, speech, and mind become inseparable from the guru's enlightened body, speech, and mind. At this point, you should meditate on mahāmudrā.

3. THE SPECIAL PRELIMINARIES

WHILE THE FOUR COMMON preliminaries are common to all schools of Buddhism, and the four uncommon preliminaries are unique to the Vajrayāna school of Buddhism, the special preliminaries are found only in the mahāmudrā teachings. There are four special preliminaries: (1) the causal condition, (2) the empowering condition, (3) the supporting condition, and (4) the immediately preceding condition. In the mahāmudrā tradition this framework is used to explain what a practitioner needs to develop in their practice.

The Causal Condition

The causal condition for spiritual practice in the mahāmudrā tradition is disciplining one's mind and developing renunciation, which is the aspiration that wishes for liberation from saṃsāra.

Discipline the mind well, and having contemplated
renunciation and the desire for liberation,
cut off all attachments and
simply remain as a renunciant in an isolated place,
without outer or inner wandering.

The essence of the Buddha's teaching is summed up in a sūtra quote that says, "Abandon negative deeds, engage in virtuous activities, and subdue the mind. This is the teaching of the Buddha." If you are following a path that is not subduing your mind, then it is not Dharma practice.

When the mind is disciplined, it naturally turns inward and no longer pursues worldly dharmas or gets carried away by negative emotions. The eight worldly dharmas are being preoccupied with the following kinds of thoughts: (1) wanting praise, (2) fearing blame, (3) wanting fame, (4) fearing disgrace, (5) wanting gain, (6) fearing loss, (7) wanting pleasure, and (8) fearing pain. Overcoming these worldly thoughts and turning the mind toward liberation through the thought of renunciation constitutes the causal condition.

Renunciation is not an external activity. It is not as simple as just changing our clothes and putting on monastic robes. Renunciation is an inner change, an inner reorientation. With this internal transformation of renunciation, you become free from the pull of things. This change in your heart *is* the causal condition. It is what moves you forward.

The Empowering Condition

The "empowering condition" for spiritual practice in the mahāmudrā tradition refers to the guidance of a qualified guru. The path to the realization of mahāmudrā consists solely in relying on the guru, an authentic spiritual guide. Only through the guidance of a qualified guru are we able to receive and put into practice the instructions necessary to progress on the path. It is due to following the guru's teachings that one is able to overcome attachment to this life and the eight worldly dharmas.

There are different types of Buddhist teachers. Here we look at four types of guru: (1) the lineage guru, (2) the guru of the Sugata's (the Buddha's) speech, (3) the guru using the symbols of appearances, and (4) the guru of ultimate dharmatā.

The Lineage Guru

From Vajradhāra down to my root guru,
a stream of blessings, oral instructions, and so forth,
has passed down uninterruptedly, one-to-one,
in an authentic lineage until reaching my guru.

A lineage guru is your own root guru who has received the blessings and oral instructions that originated with Vajradhāra and were passed down one-to-one in the unbroken chain of a correct and authentic lineage. There are so many instructions that are not contained in books but are passed down orally. A qualified guru carries the continuity of practice of all of the profound and well-preserved oral instructions. Under the guidance of such a guru who has gained realization themselves through their own effort, the student is able to attain different meditative experiences and realizations.

In this way the mahāmudrā lineage guru explains thoughts as the path: rather than abandoning thoughts, you must see all thoughts as in the nature of the dharmakāya. With perfect wisdom, you will be able to transform thoughts. Rather than abandoning negative qualities, you will be able to *transform* all negative qualities into good qualities. All confusion arises when you fail to recognize the nature of thought itself. When you recognize thought itself as the mind, and when you are able to use the mind as the path to enlightenment, this is called *nonconfusion*. If you are not able to make thought a part of your path to enlightenment, then it is merely confusion. An authentic lineage guru is someone who sees thoughts as something useful and meaningful, who is able to explain this with wisdom, and who is able to guide students properly and skillfully.

The Guru of the Sugata's Speech

Having given rise to conviction in all that the guru has taught,
by developing the experiential understanding

that it is in no way contradictory with the word of the Jina,
all scriptures will appear as instructions.

This second kind of guru is the guru of the Sugata's speech: a guru who has pointed out the nature of one's mind, resulting in a deep conviction arising in your heart, or a deep belief in whatever the guru has taught. You will thereby develop spontaneous respect for all of the teachings of the Buddha. In the verse above, the Buddha is referred to by the epithet Jina, which means "conqueror," referring to one who has vanquished the enemy of mental afflictions. You should analyze all the teachings of your guru and the words of the Buddha, and having done so, an experience will arise within you that consists of the realization of the fact that all of the Buddha's teachings of the three different vehicles are completely compatible, coming together without contradiction. As a result, all the scriptures of all three vehicles taught by the Buddha in the three turnings of the wheel of Dharma will appear to you as though they are personal instructions.

The Guru Using the Symbols of Appearances

Because [the guru] teaches the methods of the path
by means of symbols and examples,
making use of all phenomena—the outer and inner objects
of saṃsāra and nirvāṇa, including the elements
and whatever has arisen from the elements—
all things are nothing other than the guru.

The third kind of guru is the guru using the symbols of appearances. Such a guru gives instructions through special signs to show the ground, which is the dharmakāya, sugatagarbha, or dharmatā, using many different signs, symbols, and examples. Any object belonging to saṃsāra or nirvāṇa, whether mental or physical, may be used as a sign or symbol pointing to the nature of reality, and in that way, all objects can function as the guru.

Why is it that even the four elements can function as our guru? The four elements are the essence of all the things of appearances. In order to give rise to unshakable devotion, the dharmadhātu is introduced to us through different signs and examples like the earth, and for this reason, the earth is our guru. Second, the example of water helps us to develop right effort and compassion. Just as without water, our body would be dry, without compassion, we are deficient. In this way, water too is our guru. Next, with the fire of wisdom, we will be able to burn away all kinds of defilements and obscurations, and therefore fire is also our guru. And just as the wind blows everything in its path, similarly meditative experiences and realizations are also able to blow away all obscurations and show us the way. In this manner, wind too is the guru. Finally, space is everywhere; there is nothing that space does not pervade. Similarly, the guru is like space pervading everything. In this way, the five elements are the guru. Since the five elements constitute all appearances, this guru is called the guru using the symbols of appearances.

There are many methods for introducing a student to the nature of the mind, and a skillful teacher can use the world of appearances as a support for this introduction in a multitude of ways. For example, the fifteenth Karmapa had an attendant who was extremely devoted to him and had offered the Karmapa his tea every morning for many years. On this particular morning, the Karmapa asked his attendant to bring his tea, not in his usual cup, but in a special jade cup that was almost never used. As the attendant offered the tea to the Karmapa, the Karmapa swiped at the cup, knocking it to the floor and smashing it. At that moment the attendant stood there in shock. While he was in the state of shock, the Karmapa commanded him to look at his mind. The attendant's mind was in such a state that with the Karmapa's instruction he instantly saw the nature of his mind.

That reminds me of His Holiness the sixteenth Karmapa's attendant. I remember his long beard and the very dramatic and impressive style he had of offering tea. It was so respectful. However, at the end of this elaborate tea offering, the attendant would blow on His

Holiness's tea. Of course, he was blowing on the tea out of care for the Karmapa so that the tea would not be so hot as to burn him. But to blow on the Karmapa's tea might be considered a little unorthodox and disrespectful. My point is that once you have experienced an introduction to the nature of mind, no matter how dramatic, you cannot just relax. The introduction, though extremely profound, is really only the beginning. With this, you must continue moving forward in your practice and progressing in the proper way in order to stabilize the experience.

The Guru of Ultimate Dharmatā

> **Due to establishing the unmistaken realization,**
> **which is the direct perception of the nature of one's own mind**
> **in accordance with how it was introduced by the glorious guru,**
> **one also realizes the nature of reality of all phenomena.**

The fourth kind of guru is the guru of ultimate dharmatā. After having been shown the essence of mind by the guru, once you realize the essence of mind, you will be able to realize the true nature of everything. When you realize the unfindability of the mind together with its luminosity, you will begin to realize the manifold luminosity and recognize the essence of all things. That realization itself is the guru of ultimate dharmatā.

The Supporting Condition

The supporting condition is the object of meditation, which should be free from confusion or delusion.

> **One should take as the object of practice**
> **the nature of mind, which is the primordial reality that is unaltered**

by the perspectives of Buddhist and non-Buddhist philosophical views,
and which is uncorrupted by concepts,
the play of the three kāyas, thusness itself.

The unadulterated nature of reality, which is the nature of mind, should be the object of one's meditation practice. This can be understood as the play of the three kāyas. The emptiness of the mind relates to the dharmakāya, the luminosity of the mind relates to the saṃbhogakāya, and the spontaneity of the mind relates to the nirmāṇakāya. The nature of the mind is unpolluted and unobscured by both learned and innate forms of confused thought. Confusion can come from wrong views learned from both lower schools of Buddhism and non-Buddhist philosophical systems. Confusion also results from all kinds of conceptual thought. The true essence of the mind is free from all kinds of fabrication. When you meditate, just look at the mind, without trying to exaggerate or denigrate your experience through conceptual activity. It is important that you do not try to overlay some artificial understanding of emptiness or the nature of the mind onto your experience.

The Immediately Preceding Condition

Finally, the "immediately preceding condition" refers to being free from all kinds of distraction, including even the wish to engage in meditation, but instead simply resting in the wisdom of nonthought.

At the time of engaging in the actual practice,
simply sustain the essence of the ordinary mind,
which is without thought of the object of meditation or the meditator,
and which is free from the fabrications of rejecting and adopting, and hope and doubt.

The immediately preceding condition is being free from expectations. When you undertake the actual practice, you should be free of even wishing to do this or not do that in regard to your meditation. You should be free of thoughts of the agent, action, or object of meditation. You should not have expectations for good meditative experiences or hope to avoid negative meditative experiences. If thoughts do arise then don't be concerned, just be fully present and aware of the thoughts. Actually, you know you are not meditating if you fail to recognize your thoughts. Remain in the essence of the ordinary mind (*tha mal gyi shes pa*), a state which is free from thoughts of good or bad.

PART II: THE ACTUAL PRACTICE: *ŚAMATHA AND VIPAŚYANĀ*

NOW WE DISCUSS the actual practice, how to meditate in the mahāmudrā tradition, which is divided into two types of meditation: *śamatha* and *vipaśyanā*. In general, *śamatha* refers to meditation in which the mind is single-pointedly focused, whereas *vipaśyanā* refers to meditation in which the mind engages in analysis. *Śamatha* is sometimes translated as "calm abiding" or "tranquility meditation." *Vipaśyanā* is often translated as "special insight." Since these are technical words with specific meanings that describe meditation practice, I will use the original Sanskrit terms and spend some time explaining their meanings.

We can understand these two forms of meditation through the analogy of cutting a tomato with a knife. When you want to cut a tomato, you need to hold the tomato steady. Similarly, when meditating, we want to have a steady mind so that we can clearly and stably observe the object of meditation. Thus, in meditative practice we usually begin by training in the meditation of a steady mind; this is the training in śamatha meditation. In vipaśyanā meditation you use your intellect to examine the meditation object, and in mahāmudrā meditation you directly observe the internal landscape of the mind. If we stay with the metaphor of cutting a tomato, then we can say that while practicing śamatha is like holding the tomato steady, vipaśyanā is the actual cutting of the tomato.

As we advance in our meditation practice, these forms of meditation become very natural. It is like how when you first learned how to drive a car, you had to really concentrate on every aspect of driving. You have to watch the road, keep checking your speed, remember to check all your mirrors when you change lanes, remember to signal, and so forth. After some time, however, all the elements of driving integrate automatically into one activity. It is the same with meditation. With experience there comes a point where your practices of śamatha and vipaśyanā become one activity. We call this the *union of śamatha and vipaśyanā*. Although these two types of meditation look different, we ultimately bring them together as a single practice.

4. ŚAMATHA

A General Presentation of Śamatha

We begin with meditative exercises that develop concentration with the aim of training in the meditative practice of śamatha. The text first introduces a general, succinct presentation of śamatha before then going on to give a more extensive explanation. But don't let the briefness of the presentation mislead you: these instructions might be condensed, but they are very profound. These concise and pithy instructions go straight to the heart of the practice. This is often the traditional way that mahāmudrā practice is imparted from teacher to student.

The general introduction to śamatha starts with advice for what to do with your body when you engage in this practice and then gives instructions for what to do with your mind.

Crucial Points of the Body

The crucial points of the body refer
to the seven-point posture of Vairocana,
according to which one should sit on a comfortable cushion as follows:

1. feet in vajra posture,
2. hands placed evenly,
3. shoulders spread like vultures' wings,
4. neck drawn in like an iron hook,
5. spine straight like an arrow,
6. eyes focused on the space four finger-widths in front of the tip of the nose,
7. lips and teeth resting naturally, and tongue touching the upper palate.

Our posture can have a powerful effect on our mental state. The great Indian mahāsiddhas explained that there is a relationship between our posture and the quality of our meditation. They explained that there is a subtle network of channels (*nāḍis*) that run throughout our bodies and that subtle wind-like energy (*prāṇa*) courses through these channels. The wind energy that runs through these different channels is closely associated with different mental states. When we hold our bodies in different postures, this affects the alignment of the subtle channels, which then affects the movement of the subtle wind energies. In turn, the subtle energy winds have an effect on our mental states. That is because our winds are intimately connected with our thoughts, which are often described with the analogy of a horse and a rider.

The Vajrayāna Buddhist texts explain all this in great detail; they talk about seventy-two thousand channels and five main wind energies. They explain how these wind energies relate to both our destructive emotions and the different aspects of the awakened experience. As we age, the channels of our subtle body slowly deteriorate—much like our physical body, but there are different techniques for maintaining the wisdom breath. For the present purposes, what we need to understand is that when we sit in a proper meditation posture, like the one described in the verse above, we are able to place all these channels in their proper alignment so that the wind energy inside these channels can flow smoothly and without obstruction. When this happens, the elements in the body become harmonious, you feel healthier and happier, and you also become more graceful. More importantly, the smoothing out of the flow of the subtle wind energies causes discursive thoughts to naturally subside and tranquil absorption to naturally arise. Each part of the posture has an important influence on the subtle body and subtle energies. I will explain the basics of the sitting posture, and you can receive more detailed instructions directly from your guru on how these postures relate to the channels, winds, and drops.

First, we need to find a comfortable meditation seat or cushion. Nowadays, many people have a meditation cushion that is slightly higher at the back. This is very suitable since it keeps your spine straight. When we meditate, if possible, we should take the seated position known as the seven-point posture of Vairocana. I will explain each point below.

1. The first instruction is to sit in a cross-legged position called the vajra posture, with the right leg resting on the left leg. This is the posture in which many yogis are depicted when sitting in meditation. This may be difficult for people who are not flexible, since each foot rests on the thigh of the opposite leg. If this is not possible, then you can sit in half-vajra posture, with just one foot raised up on the opposite thigh and the other resting on the floor. Alternatively, you can sit cross-legged with the left leg inside, closer to your body, and the right leg outside. This modified sitting posture is known as the bodhisattva posture.
2. The next instruction is to place your hands in a meditative mudrā with the right hand resting on top of the left palm, with both palms facing upward. If you are female, according to some yogis it is better to put the left hand on top of the right palm. The tips of the thumbs touch each other gently. Your hands should be placed four finger widths below your navel; this is a special point in the subtle body in which the winds flow.
3. Your shoulders should be evenly balanced, and your elbows should not be bent. This is what is meant when the text says, "shoulders spread like vultures' wings." It is sometimes

awkward not to bend your elbows, and so the main point here is that your shoulders are level.

4. Your chin should be slightly tucked in and tilted down in order to straighten the back of your neck. But don't drop it too much, as this will round the neck. The tip of your nose and your navel should be in the same line. This is what is meant when the text says, "neck drawn in like an iron hook."
5. The next instruction is to keep your spinal column straight like an arrow. This is an important instruction since it helps with concentration and makes you feel lighter. If we slouch, then we will get drowsy.
6. Your gaze should be directed toward the space in front of you just beyond the tip of your nose. The text mentions focusing on the space four finger-widths in front of the tip of the nose. Your eyes should be still and unmoving. The shifting of your eyes stirs the mind and brings about discursive thoughts.
7. You should rest your lips and teeth naturally, and for developing śamatha it is helpful to gently touch your tongue to your upper palate. For this type of meditation, it is good to have a little space between your upper and lower teeth and to have your lips gently closed.

It is important to be careful not to hurt yourself trying to sit in this posture. If you feel pain after five minutes of sitting, then just relax again. Don't overstrain yourself. Just relax, take a walk around, have a cup of tea, or do a few prostrations. Then come back to continue sitting.

The important point here is that if our posture is not correct, this affects our subtle body, which in turn affects our mind and therefore our meditation. For example, if we are leaning to the right in our meditation posture, then it is said that our mind will become attracted to sense objects, while if we are leaning to the left, then the mind will develop more discursive thoughts. If we are leaning forward, then it is said that the mind will become agitated, and if we are leaning back, then the mind will become more distracted.

A yogin will pay careful attention not only to their posture but also to other conditions, such as their diet. If we are serious about meditation, then we should monitor our diet. We should learn which foods make our minds dull and which foods make our minds agitated. As we learn about the impact that different foods have on our mental state, we should adjust our diets accordingly. Eating just the right amount of food is also an important consideration. As most people have experienced, eating too much makes you sleepy.

Perhaps the most important condition to be attentive to is the place where you meditate. Particularly for beginners, it is important to find a quiet place for meditation. If the place is noisy, then you may not be able to concentrate at all. But once you have mastered tranquility meditation, it does not matter where you meditate, because your concentration will be so good that even loud noises and a busy environment will not distract you.

Crucial Points of the Mind

The crucial points of the mind are,
as stated according to [Tilopa's six words of advice],
"Don't recall, don't imagine, don't think,
don't meditate, don't examine, rest naturally."
Rest in uncontrived ease, without grasping to luminosity or emptiness,
single-pointedly, loosely relaxed yet without distraction,
on the essence of this momentary ordinary mind,
which is free from refuting and affirming,
rejecting and adopting, and hoping and doubting,
and free of adhering to true existence that reifies objects.

This verse is very profound. In our Kagyü tradition, Tilopa's six words of advice are used to point out the essence of mind. They are also pith instructions for how to meditate.

The first instruction is "don't recall," which means that you should not think of the past. Thinking of the past is the cause of dualistic thinking, and from that arises attachment and aversion. Many people get trapped in the past. I met a woman in Singapore who told me that she'd been angry at someone for thirty years! I said, "Forget it. You've been suffering for thirty years in a prison of your own making." Dwelling on the past is fruitless, it is like fishing from an empty riverbed.

The second instruction is "don't imagine." This means that you should not spend your meditation time thinking about the future. When you think too much about the future, then you lose touch with the present. It is said that thinking about the future is like trying to paint the face of an unborn child.

The third instruction is "don't think." This means don't even take the present moment as your object of meditation. This might be a little confusing if you previously thought that the point of meditating is to be in the present moment. That is not exactly the point of meditation. This is why it is important to have an experienced teacher guiding your meditation practice. We should also be careful not to grasp even the present moment, which is like trying to write on water. Neither should we exaggerate or denigrate whatever is occurring at the present. Do not fabricate or alter what you see, but leave things just as they are. Do not try to add or reduce, make better or worse. To do so is said to be like letting a stranger into your house.

The fourth instruction is "don't meditate." Again, this instruction might seem very strange on the face of it. What is meant here is that we do not want to meditate in a way that gets in the way of the practice. For example, we do not want to introduce an incorrect or partial understanding of emptiness into our meditation.

The fifth instruction is "don't examine." The point here is not to arrive at a destination through effortful rational analysis. As Śāntideva says, the ultimate truth is not the domain of the intellect. An object of analysis does not lie beyond the ordinary mind. Even the highest meaning that you can arrive at through analysis is not beyond thoughts but is still within the domain of language and concepts. For example, when you engage in analytical meditation, you employ various kinds of logical reasonings to inquire into the nature of reality. You may then arrive at what you understand conceptually as "emptiness." This, however, is not genuine emptiness. Genuine emptiness is beyond words, thoughts, and expressions, much like how the actual taste of chocolate cannot be expressed by words and concepts but must be experienced directly. This kind of conceptual meditation is a form of fabrication, and it is not so meaningful. Instead of investigating, you should stabilize the mind and let it be. Drop analytical effort and remain as naturally as possible.

The sixth instruction is "rest naturally." You cannot strive to change your mind to improve your mental state or affirm or deny any aspect of your experience. Don't try to adopt what you think ought to be practiced or reject what you think ought not be practiced. Don't get caught up in hopes or doubts, like hoping for good results or special meditative experiences in your practice, or else doubting yourself and your practice. Don't grasp at the true existence of your mind or any object of your awareness. You recognize the essence of mind by simply looking *through*. See directly. When a thought arises, ask yourself, "What color is this thought? What shape is this thought?" The thought will simply dissolve under analysis. Then rest in that state, allowing the thoughts to arise, abide, and cease. Don't fall into the trap of thinking about luminosity or emptiness. Just rest on the nature of mind directly.

The crucial points concerning the mind consist in following these instructions. In sum, allow the mind to be relaxed and simply look at the mind itself, without refuting or affirming, rejecting or adopting, hoping or doubting, and without grasping to things as real objects by clinging to their true existence. Rest in this state single-pointedly, without distractions, and without even grasping to luminosity or emptiness.

A Detailed Presentation of Śamatha

Now we move to the detailed presentation of how to train in śamatha, which has three phases. First, we train in settling the mind, next we work on stabilizing this mind that has been settled, and finally we employ practices for enhancing the mind that has been stabilized.

Settling the Mind That Has Not Been Settled

When training in settling the mind, there are three different approaches that you might take. We can take up an object as our focus of meditation, or we can meditate without an object, or else we can use the breath as a point of focus.

Concentrating with an Object

We will next begin the explanation for the meditative training of settling the mind through using an object of focus. You can either use an external or internal object of focus. External objects can be physical objects that you focus on with opened eyes or objects that are visualized as outside of you. Internal objects are generally objects that you visualize inside your body. The text begins with instructions on stabilizing the mind by using an external object of focus, which is divided into two categories: ordinary objects and extraordinary objects. We'll start with concentrating on ordinary objects.

> **Sit observing the proper gaze and the crucial points of the body.**
> **Rest in single-pointed meditative equipoise,**
> **and without wandering to any other object,**
> **fix the mind on some coarse object in front of you, like a pillar or the wall.**
>
> **Similarly, concentrate without wandering on some small object**
> **in front of you, like a stick or a pebble.**
> **Moreover, you can concentrate by taking as your focal object**
> **a candle flame, space, or similarly**
> **a pea-sized white drop at the point between the brows.**

There are many different ordinary objects that you can take as an initial object of meditation in order to develop a steadier meditative experience. You can begin by choosing a large and unmoving external object, like a wall in front of you. Once you are able to remain focused on this object without allowing the mind to wander, you can progressively move to smaller objects, like a pebble or a small stick placed in front of you. Then when you are able to meditate well utilizing a smaller object of focus, you can focus on an even subtler object, such as a candle flame, the space in front of you, or a visualized white dot located at the point between the brows.

You can get more details on how to take these subtle objects as the focus of your meditation from a qualified teacher. I will explain them briefly to give you an idea of the practice.

First sit with the proper gaze, observing the crucial points of the body, the seven-point posture of Vairocana, as discussed above.

To take a candle flame as the object of meditation, place a candle on your right or left side where the wind is not blowing, and place a very clean mirror in front of you in such a way that you can see the reflection of the candle in the mirror. Then focus on the reflection of the flame in the mirror.

To use the space in front of you as the object of meditation, begin by focusing on a very small space between your thumbs. Next, you can expand your focus to the space in your room. Then, expand your focus even more to a vast space that encompasses mountains, rivers, and so forth. Finally, you can focus on the entirety of space, encompassing the whole universe. Actually, the instruction is to expand your focus to encompass the three realms: the form realm, the formless realm, and the desire realm.

When using a white dot as the object of meditation, focus on the center of the forehead where the bone forms a triangle, since it is said that consciousness gathers at this point. Then visualize a very tiny white-colored dot, the size of a single grain.

You can also take an extraordinary object as the object of your meditation. An extraordinary object, also known as a pure object, is something associated with awakening rather than something mundane. The example in the verse below is the form of the Buddha.

> **Visualize in front of you the complete Buddha, the Bhagavan,**
> **together with the appropriate color, clothing, marks, and signs,**
> **and hold the mind there**
> **with reverence, single-pointedly.**

It is said that meditating with faith and devotion on a pure object, like the form of the Buddha, can amplify your good qualities. To practice in this way, focus on an image of Śākyamuni Buddha, or one of the other buddhas, in the space in front of you, with the appropriate color and clothing, and adorned with the thirty-two major marks and eighty minor signs. Visualize the Buddha with both clarity and devotion, and rest the mind single-pointedly.

The next set of instructions are to visualize an internal object, meaning an object within you, as the focus for your meditation.

> **Generate whichever yidam is appropriate, or meditate on your guru**
> **seated on an eight-petaled lotus at your heart,**
> **or else visualize a luminous ball of light**
> **that is in essence your yidam or guru and hold the mind on it.**
>
> **Without wandering from these focal objects,**
> **maintain the proper gaze and be free of the faults too tight and too loose.**

Apart from the spy of mindfulness, remain in a state that is free of construction.
Without rejecting or adopting, hoping or doubting,
rest the mind just as it is, loosely relaxed, lightly, and unrestrained.

With this meditation you visualize a lotus with eight petals inside your chest at the level of your heart. At the center of the lotus, visualize your yidam or guru, or a ball of light that is in nature your yidam or guru. If you are unable to visualize your yidam because it is too complicated, then simply visualize a white light that radiates out from the lotus and think that this light emanates from the yidam. The light should be pure white and very luminous. Use this as the focus of your meditation, and do not allow your mind to wander.

Just as to be comfortable throughout the day, your pants belt should not be too tight or too loose, in meditation our concentration should not be too tight or too loose. Sit in proper meditation posture and focus on the visualization, free from the faults of holding the object too loosely or too tightly. Once you have settled on the object, do not make efforts to try to improve or diminish your experience in any respect, and do not allow your mind to get caught up in thoughts of rejecting or adopting, hope or worry, doubt, etc. Remain in this way, allowing the mind to rest just as it is, loose, lightly, and unrestrained.

Concentrating without an Object

Now we move to the second type of practice for settling the mind: meditating without a specific object of focus.

Concentrate instantaneously on the great emptiness
of all phenomena, both outer and inner objects,
or else dissolve those objects one into the other,
and set the mind in meditative equipoise on the great emptiness and luminosity.

When concentrating without an object, you can focus on the emptiness of all internal and external objects, meaning all mental and physical things in their entirety. See the entirety of external and internal objects as simply emptiness. Alternatively, you can visualize that all things dissolve one into another, from one element to the next, until everything has dissolved into emptiness. Then rest in meditative equipoise on the fact that everything is empty yet luminous. Without any focus, rest on that nature. When you focus in such a way, you may see or hear something special, but if you allow yourself to develop attachment to any of your meditative experiences, then although such an experience may have been praiseworthy, your attachment will diminish it. Thus, it is important not to have attachment and to see everything as an illusion.

Concentrating on the Breath

Next is the third type of practice for settling the mind: meditating on the breath.

> **To concentrate on the breath, focus on vase-breathing,**
> **or count the rounds of breath up to twenty-one, and so on,**
> **counting each exhalation, inhalation, and retention as a single breath.**
> **Strive for a long time with many repetitions without wandering,**
> **maintaining clarity, lucidity, and intensity.**
>
> **In that way, by meditating according to these oral instructions,**
> **the following three stages will successively arise:**
> **the first is like a waterfall on a cliff face,**
> **the second is like a gently flowing river,**
> **and the third is like an unfluctuating ocean.**

To concentrate on the breath, engage in vase breathing: hold the breath and energy gently in your stomach after you inhale. If you become uncomfortable, then simply let it go. This is not the more intensive vase breathing where you pull up and push down while holding the wind four finger-widths below the navel. Instead, simply focus on the exhale, then inhale, and then gently hold the breath, imagining that it remains four finger-widths below the navel. Alternatively, you can pull the energy down but without pulling up. This is less intensive. If you practice this a lot, it is said that you will have a lot of energy and will be able to run quickly. If you feel that your wind and energy is stagnant, it is important to clear it in order to avoid injury. To do this, you can forcefully exhale several times through the nose and extend the fingers at the same time with each exhale. To engage in these last few meditations it is crucial to have the guidance of a qualified teacher.

Stabilizing the Mind That Has Been Settled

Once you have settled the mind through the practices just described, next train in the second of the three phases for training in śamatha: stabilizing the mind that has been settled. For example, once you have recognized the nature of the mind, you do not want to lose this recognition, so the second phase of this meditation instruction is to maintain this recognition of the mind through various techniques. The goal is to stabilize the recognition of the mind.

There are two kinds of methods to stabilize the mind that has been settled. The first method for stabilizing the mind is called holding the mind, and the second is the well-known ninefold method for resting the mind.

Holding the Mind

There are three different techniques for holding the mind. The first is holding the mind above, the second is holding the mind below, and the third is the yoga of alternating, which is alternating between the first two techniques of holding the mind above and holding the mind below.

The next verse gives the instructions for holding the mind above.

Focus the mind and hold the wind within a pea-sized white drop
in the center of a four-petaled lotus at the heart.
As you expel the wind, the drop goes out through the aperture of Brahmā
and imagine that it remains in the expanse of space.

Strive at maintaining the proper gaze
and the crucial points of the body.
Uplift the mind and intensify your awareness;
in that way, meditate for a long time.

To engage in the technique of holding the mind above, begin by adopting the seven-point meditation posture and relaxing the mind. Then visualize a four-petaled white lotus at your heart. In the center of this lotus imagine a white drop about the size of a pea. The drop is oily in appearance and shining like mercury.

Focus on this white drop. Then on your inhale, hold the breath, and imagine that the breath, which represents the inner winds, is held in this white drop. Now when you are ready to exhale, forcefully expel the breath, and visualize that the white drop is ejected from your crown. Imagine that the white drop is propelled very high into space. Cultivate an uplifted mental state and remain concentrated on that drop. Be sure to maintain the correct seven-point meditation posture throughout as you maintain this focus.

Any time that you are holding the breath during meditation practice, and especially when holding the breath while maintaining focus at the heart area, you need to be careful to avoid what in the tradition is thought of as a wind disorder. This is one of the reasons that it is best to do these practices under the guidance of an experienced teacher. This technique will help you to correctly stabilize your meditation practice. It is a particularly helpful technique for overcoming dullness in your meditation.

When the verse mentions the aperture of Brahmā, it is referring to the crown of your head. This technique is also called "the meditation of Brahmā's crown." It is also the best practice for meditating on the Akaniṣṭha pure realm.

The next verse discusses the second technique: holding the mind below.

> **The second holding: in the center of a downward-facing**
> **four-petaled black lotus is a pea-sized black drop.**
> **Like the thread drawn from a spider, it spirals down**
> **and is drawn out from the secret place.**
> **It gradually descends, remaining heavily many fathoms**
> **beneath you.**
> **Hold the mind single-pointedly on that, contract the anus,**
> **and meditate maintaining the crucial points of the body**
> **and a downward gaze.**

To practice the technique of holding the mind below, once again take the seven-point meditation posture and relax the mind, but this time visualize a four-petaled black lotus in your heart. The lotus is facing downward, and in the center of the lotus is a black drop about the size of a pea. Then, imagine that the drop begins to descend slowly. According to the verse, the drop descends like a thread drawn from the body of a spider who is weaving a web. The drop is drawn out from your secret organ and gradually descends many miles beneath the earth. It is important to imagine the black drop as heavy and hanging from a string. Hold the mind single-pointedly on that drop and constrict the anal sphincter. Ensure that you continually maintain the proper meditation posture and allow your gaze to rest downward. This technique will help you correctly stabilize your meditation practice. It is a particularly helpful technique for overcoming agitation in your meditation.

Next is the third technique for holding the mind above and below, which is the yoga of alternating.

Moreover, according to your assessment,
if your mind is too elevated, then hold below,
and if your mind is too low, then hold above.
Alternate the practice using these two focal objects [as appropriate],
continually making effort, like the flow of a river.

The final technique for holding the mind requires you to first determine the quality of your meditation and then to apply the previous two techniques as necessary. The verse advises, "if your mind is too elevated, then hold below." This description of the mind as elevated refers to a mind that is too active. When you check the quality of your meditation, if you find that your mind is agitated or too active, then you should apply the method for holding the mind below. This practice can also help if you are developing pride in your meditation, by promoting the development of humility.

The verse continues, saying, "if your mind is too low, then hold above." When it describes the mind as low, it is referring to a mind that is dull. When you check the quality of your meditation, if you find that your mind is dull, then follow the instructions for holding the mind above. This technique can also help if your practice is uninspired.

Another helpful instruction to apply is that if your mind is too active, then you should lower your meditative gaze, and if your mind is too dull, then you should raise your meditative gaze.

Monitor your meditation practice and apply these techniques for holding the mind to improve the stability of your meditation according to your experience. If you make continual efforts at the application of these techniques, you will find that the quality of your meditation improves and becomes consistent. Your meditative experience will become very smooth and continuous like the flow of water in a river.

Ninefold Method for Resting the Mind

The other set of instructions for stabilizing the mind that has been settled is called the nine stages for resting the mind.

(1) Placement, (2) continuous placement, (3) definite
placement,
(4) close placement, (5) disciplining, (6) pacifying,
(7) thoroughly pacifying, (8) creating a single continuum,
and (9) even placement.

The meaning of these is taught in succession:

1. [Placement:] Place the mind, fixing it single-pointedly on the focal object.
2. [Continuous placement:] Settle the mind on that object for a long time.
3. [Definite placement:] If thoughts arise, recognize that with your mindfulness immediately, and place the mind evenly.
4. [Close placement:] Place the mind evenly by mixing the mind of meditative equipoise with the previously settled mind.
5. [Disciplining:] Recalling the virtues of the settled mind, develop joy, and remain in that state.
6. [Pacifying:] Ascertain which conditions give rise to wandering, overcome attachment to those, and remain so.
7. [Thoroughly pacifying:] Recognize the nature of the causes of distraction and unhappiness, etc., and simply self-liberate them.
8. [Creating a single continuum:] Having meditated in that way, remain engaged with the focal object spontaneously and without depending on effort.
9. [Even placement:] Finally, be free of all distractions about whether or not one is in equipoise.

It is helpful to explain the stages of the ninefold method for resting the mind based on meditating with the support of an object of focus:

1. Placement: Place the mind on whatever focal object you have taken up and fix the mind on it single-pointedly. At first, the length of time you are able to stay on the object without wandering off and thinking about some other topic will be very short, but with practice it will start to lengthen.
2. Continuous placement: Maintain placement on your focal object continuously for as long as you can. As the length of time you are able to hold the object of meditation increases, you reach the second stage, which is known as "continuous placement." At this stage you are better able to maintain concentration on the object.
3. Definite placement: If thoughts arise, catch them with the tool of mindfulness and place the mind back on the object. When you are able to keep your concentration on the object for a short amount of time, you then must begin to make efforts to keep the continuity of concentration to ensure that you are not drifting away from your object of meditation. When you start noticing that you have forgotten your object of meditation, quickly place your mind back on the object.
4. Close placement: Whenever the mind is fully focused, mix that mind with the previously settled mind. Here, forgetting the object of meditation is no longer much of a problem, but continued effort is made to improve the quality of the concentration so that it is stable.
5. Disciplining: Recall the qualities of residing in meditation with concentration, and with a joyful mind, continue to meditate in that state of joy. At this stage, you take delight in improving your meditation practice through reflecting upon the advantages of meditation. With this it becomes easier to deal with distractions and dullness.
6. Pacifying: Whenever your mind starts to wander, recognize that it is wandering in saṃsāra. See saṃsāra as a place of suffering, develop disinterest in saṃsāra, and remain as long as possible in that state. At this stage, through reflecting on the

disadvantages of wasting your time, distraction toward objects of the senses is diminished such that as soon as they arise, they are noticed and pacified.

7. Thoroughly pacifying: The causes of wandering thoughts are mental afflictions like covetousness, maliciousness, and wrong views. Due to these, our mind state becomes very unpleasant. When you look at the causes and effects of all these poisons, they will become self-liberated, dissolving in themselves, since they have no essence or properties to be found. At this stage, not only are we overcoming subtle disturbances created by attachment to the objects of the senses, but we are also able to immediately eliminate any emotions that arise, such as worry. We should recognize the cause of all of these hindrances and also reflect upon the trouble that hindrances bring us.
8. Creating a single continuum: Having meditated in that way, your focus will naturally develop, and you will continuously remain in such a meditative state.
9. Even placement: When you have reached equipoise through this technique, without any effort, all active and inactive minds will dissolve by themselves, and you will be able to remain in equipoise.

Once we have recognized the nature of the mind, we then need to stabilize it. When we gain proficiency in stabilizing this mind, we next work to enhance this mind. So, now we turn to the enhancement practices.

Enhancing the Mind That Has Been Stabilized

Once you have settled the mind, and then stabilized the mind that has been settled, you then move on to the third phase of training in śamatha: enhancing the mind that has been stabilized.

> **Focus your awareness on the forms of visual appearances, and likewise, taking sound, etc., in succession**

as your focal support, place the mind single-pointedly.
Moreover, whatever conceptual thoughts arise,
place the mind on them directly without viewing them as faults.
Alternately apply tightening and loosening,
and in particular, dispel obstacles and make progress.
Pray to the guru, and through your devotion,
the guru's mind and your own mind will become mixed as one.

The technique for enhancing the mind that has been stabilized begins with taking the objects of the five senses in turn as the focal objects of your meditation. You start with focusing on forms appearing as visual objects, and then move to sounds, smells, tastes, and tangible objects. After gaining experience with taking the objects of the five senses as the focal object of your meditation, you then move on to taking thoughts themselves as your object of meditation.

Whatever thoughts arise, directly observe them without trying to manipulate them. For this technique we can categorize thoughts into three types: (1) those that should be discarded, (2) those that should be adopted, and (3) those that are neutral. No matter which type of thoughts arise, do not think of them as problems or something that should be discarded. Instead simply look at the thoughts themselves, just as they are. Watch whatever thoughts arise, whether they are thoughts that we would usually attempt to eliminate, or thoughts that we would usually strive to cultivate, or neutral thoughts.

Having taken thoughts themselves as the object of our meditation, we need to examine the quality of our meditative experience. So, the next instruction in the verse advises us to check to see whether we need to tighten or loosen our mind. This means that we should be aware of and monitor any changes in our meditative experience. For example, if the mind becomes too loose, then we need to apply the technique of tightening our focus, and if the mind becomes too tight, then we need to apply the technique of loosening our focus. *Tightening* means maintaining constant effort to hold the mind firmly on the object, and *loosening* means allowing the mind to be more relaxed as it holds its object.

When the mind is too loose, it will become dull, so you should practice tightening to counteract dullness. This means that you should not allow your mind to wander even for a second. It's as if your mouth, eyes, and ears are all standing at attention and you are on the edge of your seat, as though engrossed in a movie. This kind of mental focus is like tightrope walking, or like trying to walk very carefully while balancing a bowl of butter on your head. It is also similar to the situation of heightened awareness that you may develop while you are in the market and you know that a thief is lurking. Among the many people crowding the shops, you will single out and focus on the thief alone.

If, on the other hand, the mind becomes too tight, then it will grow agitated, so you should then practice loosening. Loosening means allowing the mind to be more relaxed as it holds its object. This does not mean losing the object, as mindfulness is thoroughly preserved. Prolong the time of the meditation session a little but maintain a relaxed mind. The feeling of a relaxed mind is like when you cut the thread on a bundle of straw, or like the sun and moon unobscured by clouds, or a candle undisturbed by the wind.

Here the thoughts themselves are not the problem; it is the dullness and agitation of the mind that are obstacles to our practice of śamatha. It is the quality of mind that observes the thought that is being monitored and corrected. If we are not observing the thoughts with clarity and are getting lost in the thoughts, then this is not the optimal meditation state. So, we should remove all internal and external obstacles. External obstacles are distractions that arise due to sounds and other sense objects. Internal obstacles are the variety of thoughts and mental disturbances, such as agitation and dullness, that may distract you or impede your progress. In order to meditate well, you should be able to overcome these hindrances and challenges. You have to be especially careful with dullness, since if you fall into the trap of this unfavorable condition, there is the danger that even though you might think your meditation is getting better, it is actually getting worse. A good short session is much better than a long session characterized by dullness. For beginners, one should always begin with short sessions. Gradually, you should work at prolonging your meditation sessions as long as you can maintain the quality of the meditation session.

The real secret to enhancing your meditation has to do with devotion. Through your devotion and through the practice of guru yoga, your own mind and the guru's mind will become mixed as if inseparable. There's a saying: whoever has the best devotion has the best meditation, whoever has middling devotion has middling meditation, and whoever has poor devotion has poor meditation. Likewise, if someone has no devotion at all, they will have no meditation. So, in order to progress in mahāmudrā meditation, you must develop devotion.

5. VIPAŚYANĀ

WE HAVE FINISHED the instructions on śamatha, or calm abiding, and we now move to the instructions on vipaśyanā, or insight meditation. The vipaśyanā instructions will be broken up into three main sections. The first section will take up the subject of looking at the nature of reality, the essence of mind. It is difficult to get an actual taste of the essence of the mind, and so in the second section, called "Cutting the Fundamental Root," we will look at the meditator and activity of looking at the essence of the mind. Finally, the third section addresses introduction to the nature of mind by means of determining awareness to be empty.

LOOKING AT THE NATURE OF REALITY, THE ESSENCE OF MIND

The way to look at the nature of reality, the essence of mind,
is to place the mind loosely, relaxed, just as it is, and without fabrication.
Examine and analyze [its] essence, color, shape, and so forth, looking again and again.

The essence of the resting [mind]
should be luminous and naked, vivid alertness.
If, having searched for the resting [mind], you do not find it,
let it be free and analyze how it fluctuates.

This practice of looking at the nature of the mind is not a practice in which you are trying to manipulate the quality of your mental state. Instead, you look directly at the mind itself. You look directly at the mind, leaving it just as it is, without trying to make it better or worse. Remain relaxed without tightness. Look at the mind again and again, however it is residing. Then begin analyzing the way in which the essence of mind has no color, no shape, etc. When you look at the mind at rest, you will find it to be luminous. See the naked, raw image of the mind. Actually, the nature of the mind cannot really be put into words. We can say things like the mind is luminous, but this is only an expression. We can say that we see the naked body of the mind, but again, this is obviously just an expression.

If you cannot find stability during this process, then let the mind wander, and again try to analyze this wandering mind. Observe and analyze the mind in stillness and the mind wandering. These instructions are a form of introduction to the nature of the mind. It is important that you are guided by a lineage teacher so that you do not develop a misunderstanding about the instructions on showing the nature of the mind.

When analyzing the mind, if you cannot find the mind, then the instruction is to look at the person who is analyzing. This moves us to the second instruction on vipaśyanā: cutting the fundamental root.

Cutting the Fundamental Root

Then, as for showing how to cut the fundamental root:
when you search but do not find [the mind],

search again and again by properly analyzing
the searcher and how the mind arises, abides, and departs,
etc.

Moreover, the eleven mental applications are
(1) thorough searching, (2) individual examination, (3) detailed analysis,
(4) śamatha, (5) vipaśyanā, (6) union [of śamatha and vipaśyanā],
(7) clarity, (8) nonconceptuality, (9) equanimity,
(10) uninterrupted continuity, (11) nondistraction.

The meaning of these is taught respectively as follows:

1. [Thorough searching:] Search continuously for the mental continuum, [inquiring,] "Does the mind exist or not, and what is its essence like?"
2. [Individual examination:] In particular, cut the fundamental root,
   [examining] the color, shape, etc., the arising, abiding, departing, and the foundation.
3. [Detailed analysis:] Search for the ultimate status of that which is sought and the searcher.
4. [Śamatha:] Having realized that the mind has no nature by having searched for it,
   in order to determine the nature of reality of all phenomena as well,
   rest the mind on the profound meaning.
5. [Vipaśyanā:] By searching for the essence of that previous resting itself, thoroughly realize the very nature.
6. [Union of śamatha and vipaśyanā:] Those two are nondistinct and indistinguishable.

7. **[Clarity:] If you become dull and drowsy,
then stimulate and uplift the mind.**
8. **[Nonconceptuality:] If you become scattered and agitated,
then strive at the methods of pacification.**
9. **[Equanimity:] Once you have become free of dullness and agitation,
rest in the essence of [the mind that was] sought, examined, and analyzed.**
10. **[Uninterrupted continuity:] Never be separated from such a practice.**
11. **[Nondistraction:] Having concentrated the mind on this,
wandering will never find an opportunity.**

By means of these eleven mental applications, exert yourself again and again at the method for cutting the fundamental root.

If you find the instructions for analyzing the mind to be difficult, and if you are not gaining certainty in your experience on the nature of mind, then start to look for the one who is analyzing. Where is the analyzing coming from? Where is this looking mind coming from, where does it abide, and where does it go? Then, if the mind resides calmly, look at that. Or if the mind becomes active, look at that.

There are eleven mental applications that can be used to analyze the mind so as to cut the fundamental root itself. I will touch on each very briefly.

1. Thorough searching: With this technique, we search continuously for the mental continuum, inquiring whether the mind exists or not, leaving no stone unturned.
2. Individual examination: This is a coarse kind of analysis, which involves trying to discern the shape, color, form, etc., of

the mind, together with trying to ascertain where the mind is coming from, where it remains, and where it goes.

3. Detailed analysis: This is a more subtle and detailed analysis, which involves inquiring into the ultimate nature of the object that is searched for and the searcher themselves. You will find that they are empty.
4. Śamatha: Having realized that the mind is devoid of any nature through having searched for it, come to realize the nature of reality of all phenomena by resting the mind on the profound meaning that was arrived at through inquiring into the nature of mind.
5. Vipaśyanā: Whenever you reside in the essence of the mind as arrived at before, upon searching you realize the true reality of the mind completely.
6. Union of śamatha and vipaśyanā: At this point, you realize that the essence of mind and the mind itself are indivisible.
7. Clarity: If your mind becomes dull, then think of what makes your mind active and uplift your mind.
8. Nonconceptuality: If your mind becomes too active, then utilize one of the methods for calming your mind.
9. Equanimity: When you are able to remain free of both agitation and dullness, you should simply rest in the essence of the mind that was sought.
10. Uninterrupted continuity: Make effort to engage in this practice continuously so that you are never separated from it.
11. Nondistraction: Finally, maintain total focus, since if your mind is always focused on such practices, the wandering mind will never find a moment to distract you.

With these eleven methods, one should try to understand the essence of the mind and all phenomena deeply within, and thereby cut the fundamental root of ignorance itself.

Here we have come to the introduction to the empty nature of *rigpa*, or awareness: the pointing out of the emptiness of awareness itself. This is called *introduction* because the practitioner is shown what it means for awareness to be empty.

There are different methods for showing that awareness is empty for different kinds of practitioners. Dividing practitioners by their capacities, there are three kinds: the simultaneist (*chikcharwa*), the bypasser (*thögalwa*), and the gradualist (*rimgyipa*).

These days, simultaneist practitioners are extremely rare. These practitioners are able to instantly achieve high levels of realization based simply on the pith instructions, or through certain gestures or signs given by a realized guru. Such a practitioner has a strong devotion to the guru, has eradicated all kinds of acts of nonvirtue, and has diminished their obscurations. Such a person can experience something that is beyond expression at the very moment of introduction to the mind. The example used to illustrate this kind of inexpressible realization, or experience, is that of a mute person tasting some very delicious food. The person has a very real, intense experience of the taste of the food but is unable to describe it.

Certain advanced students who are under the guidance of an authentic and powerful guru can possibly attain one of the four yogas instantly: single-pointedness, freedom from elaborations, one taste, and nonmeditation. I will be explaining these stages later. And when they attain one of the higher levels, all of the lower realizations are gained automatically. For example, if the guru gives this type of student the introduction to the nature of their awareness, then the student may even achieve the fourth yoga, the yoga of nonmeditation. Despite not having gone through the stages one by one, upon attaining the realization of the yoga of nonmeditation, all the realizations from the three lower yogas—single-pointedness, freedom from elaborations, one taste—are also recognized. In this way, it is possible for all the qualities of all four levels to be acquired instantaneously. These days, this is extremely rare.

There are other types of practitioners who are at times able to "bypass," or skip, some stages of the path due to practice in previous lives, but they are not able to maintain those levels of experience. For instance, a bypasser might instantly have a realization of śamatha and then later might struggle to develop śamatha. Or they might even have some level of vipaśyanā without śamatha, and then later might not have an experience of either. These types of practitioners are called "bypassers."

The vast majority of students are gradualist practitioners. Due to the lack of prior practice or purification, these students must practice śamatha and vipaśyanā gradually, in the proper sequence of the stages of traversing the path, so that realization gradually arises.

Introduction by Determining Awareness to Be Empty

You must make a request to the guru for this instruction. When introduction is given, a basis is required. So, you should sit in meditation posture and do not allow your mind to wander but remain fully focused. Then try to rest in the nature of mind. Look at the mind itself directly. Make sure that the continuity of this is thoroughly present. Thoughts may arise or cease, but just let them be without trying to make them better or worse. Those who have broken samaya cannot be present for these instructions.

As for the method of introduction by determining awareness to be empty:
Firstly, relax and rest the mind in its natural state.
Look nakedly at the essence of the relaxed mind.
Rely continuously on mindfulness that is completely undistracted.

No matter what conceptual thoughts arise,
do not engage in any kind of fabrication, including rejecting and adopting.
Rest with lucid alertness on the momentary ordinary mind,
the ungraspable, vivid wakefulness of luminous emptiness.

Relax and look nakedly at the essence of the relaxed mind and rely continuously on mindfulness that is without distraction. Do not try to make the mind or any thoughts that arise better or worse. Look at the ordinary mind. You will see that there is nothing that you can pinpoint. The mind is empty yet luminous. That is how you must remain.

As for the manner of introduction, there are two divisions: (1) introduction on the basis of movement, and (2) introduction on the basis of appearance.

Introduction on the Basis of Movement

Next, the instruction is to look at the mind when it is moving, wandering, or engaged in any conceptual thought. Try to pinpoint the nature of mind while the mind is wandering, and based on that, the nature of the mind is recognized.

> **Moreover, as for the method of introduction on the basis of movement,**
> **initially, rest awareness loosely in its natural state.**
> **From within that state, look at its essence.**
> **Then, bring about [mental] movement, and once more [inquire],**
> **"What is the difference between the moving mind and the resting mind?"**
> **Through looking for the difference between**
> **the moving mind and the mind that is looking at it,**
> **the movement is self-liberated.**
> **Rest single-pointedly in that state without wandering.**

Initially, the mind should be fully relaxed. Let it reside in its own nature. From that nature, look at the essence of mind. Then allow the mind to be active and wander as it will, and at that moment, focus on the mind that is wandering. Investigate the mind that wanders, inquiring into what the difference is between the mind that wanders and the mind that remains at rest. When you look at it directly, even the wandering mind will dismantle itself. This is called self-liberation. Remain in this state.

Introduction on the Basis of Appearance

The stages of insight based on recognition of the nature of mind are the insight (1) that all appearances are mind, (2) that the mind itself is empty, (3) that emptiness is spontaneous, and (4) that spontaneity is self-liberated. Each of these four aspects can be taken as a basis of introduction to the nature of mind and reality, and these aspects are used to explain the introduction on the basis of appearance.

Introducing Appearance as the Mind

> **By examining whether mind and its**
> **focal objects, such as forms, are the same or different,**
> **once you realize that all objects appearing as external are not established**
> **as anything other than the natural radiance of the mind,**
> **rest openly in that state without grasping.**

Are the objects that appear to the mind the same as the mind or different from the mind? Are the mind and its appearance one thing, two things, or many things? Examine the appearing forms and the mind, inquiring into whether they are identical or distinct.

When you analyze in this way, what you find is that all that you see as external is merely the reflection of the mind. There is nothing that really exists externally, because whatever appears is inseparable from the mind. Having realized that all appearing objects that seem to be external things are inseparable from the mind, rest the mind loosely in the state of that realization without grasping.

Introducing Mind Itself as Empty

Mind itself is not established at all but is emptiness.
It cannot be conveyed by any means.
It is beyond words, thoughts, and expression, like space.
Rest naturally in that state without fabricating.

The mind itself does not really exist as any definitive property that can be pinpointed. Its nature cannot be articulated or defined by any means. The nature of the mind is beyond words, beyond thoughts, and beyond expression, like space. How much can you really say about the qualities of space as the mere absence of obstruction? Mind itself is not established; so, we can say it is empty. Remain in the state of this experience without engaging in the mental fabrication of conceptual thought.

Introducing Emptiness as Spontaneous

Unmoving from the empty dharmatā,
the unceasing expressivity and radiance in fact dawns as the variety [of appearances].
All the phenomenal appearances of saṃsāra and nirvāṇa are nothing other than emptiness.
Spontaneity should be known as the inseparability of appearance and emptiness.

To say that the mind is empty obviously does not mean that the mind is static or inert. The mind is empty, like space, and yet without moving from such empty nature, it is luminous and spontaneous. All the phenomena of saṃsāra and nirvāṇa are spontaneously arisen, and yet all this spontaneously arisen appearance is not beyond emptiness. Whatever appears is empty, whatever is empty is an appearance. You must realize the union of appearance and emptiness.

Introducing Spontaneity as Self-Liberated

Likewise, the three of appearance, awareness, and emptiness
have primordially been the spontaneity of the union of luminosity and emptiness.
Without relying on the antidotes of adopting or discarding, eliminating or adding,
that ultimate self-liberation is mahāmudrā.

These three—appearance, awareness, and emptiness—are from the beginning luminous yet empty. They are beginningless, self-arisen oneness. When you realize this nature, all misperceptions will be cleared away. Rest in that state without abandoning or adopting, and without depending on an antidote. This is the actual self-liberation, which is mahāmudrā.

This is a very profound instruction and I am just giving you a taste here. Please practice the foundational practices well and seek the direct guidance from a lineage master. Do not fall prey to the many traps along the path that lie in wait for those guided only by books.

PART III: CONCLUSION

ONCE THE STUDENT HAS been introduced to the nature of their mind and has gained some meditative experience, four additional points are taught: (1) how to develop one's capacity and make progress, (2) how to eliminate obstacles, (3) how to traverse the path, and (4) how to actualize the result. First, we will look at how one develops their capacity.

6. HOW TO DEVELOP ONE'S CAPACITY AND MAKE PROGRESS

THE TEACHING ON HOW to develop your capacity has four parts. It begins with the way to make spiritual progress through dispelling five misconceptions. Having first explained how to overcome the five misconceptions, the text then moves on to the three skills to be trained in to progress along the path. Having explained the three skills, the text moves on to explain how to avoid certain deviations and pitfalls in one's meditation practice. Finally, it is explained how to make progress through crossing the three dangerous passes.

Making Progress by Dispelling the Five Misconceptions

The five misconceptions are (1) misconceptions about the object, (2) misconceptions about time, (3) misconceptions with respect to the essence, (4) misconceptions with respect to the nature, and (5) misconceptions with respect to knowledge. The next five verses take us through these five misconceptions.

How to Eliminate Misconceptions with Respect to the Object

Through taking all phenomena included within dualism—
such as the object to be abandoned, saṃsāra,
and the object to be accomplished, nirvāṇa,
fixation and nongrasping, virtue and vice, etc.—
to be of an equal taste in the sphere of nondual wisdom,
one eliminates misconceptions with respect to objects.

This verse addresses a misconception in relation to objects and our perception of objects, particularly those objects and ideas that are considered a part of the Buddhist path. For example, it is generally taught that we should seek to abandon the causes for our continued suffering in saṃsāra and that we should instead strive to attain nirvāṇa. For instance, we are often advised to avoid all forms of wrongdoing and undertake the practice of virtue. Yet, if we undertake these activities with a dualistic misconception that imagines appearances to have some substantial, mind-independent status, then we will make only limited progress. In order to dispel the misconceptions with respect to objects, we must gain an experience of the understanding that all these dualistic dharmas are in fact of a single taste with the sphere of nondual wisdom. In this way, we can eradicate the thought of subject and object, or perceiver and percept.

How to Eliminate Misconceptions with Respect to Time

While the three times are not truly established,
the division of the three times is imputed by delusion.
Thus, given that the three times are not established as distinct,
through realizing their equality,
one eliminates misconceptions with respect to time.

Our wrong conceptions about time make up the second kind of misconception that we must overcome to progress along the spiritual path. We seem to experience the present as a very vivid and real thing. We talk about the past and the future as if they exist in some very accessible way, whether through memory or imagination. However, if you examine very carefully and look for the present, look for the past, look for the future, then you will discover that the three times are unfindable. They cannot be pinned down. You will instead find that the three times are not truly established. The conceptual fabrication of the three times is simply a label that we employ due to our ignorance. The three times never existed separately or distinct from one another. They are all one in nature. When you completely realize this, you will be free from misconceptions with respect to time.

How to Eliminate Misconceptions with Respect to the Essence

It is incorrect to assert that wisdom is obtained
subsequent to renouncing the present mind.
Through understanding that one's mind has been primordially
in the nature of the five wisdoms,
one eliminates misconceptions with respect to the essence.

The fourth misconception to overcome in order to progress along the spiritual path is the misunderstanding about the essence of the mind. If you wish to become a buddha, you cannot renounce the mind, because the essence of the mind itself is wisdom. From beginningless time, the essence of mind has never been different from the five wisdoms. By knowing this, one will become free from misconceptions with respect to the essence of mind.

How to Eliminate Misconceptions with Respect to the Nature

All the aggregates, constituents, and sense spheres of all sentient beings exist

in the nature of the tathāgatas, male and female, gods and goddesses.
Through understanding this,
one eliminates misconceptions with respect to the nature.

We must also overcome misconceptions regarding the nature of the things that make up our world. This is the fourth misconception to overcome to progress along the path. All the five aggregates (*skandhas*), twelve sense spheres (*āyatanas*), and eighteen constituents (*dhātus*) of all sentient beings are in the nature of the male and female buddhas and yidam deities. When you realize this, you will be free from misconceptions with respect to the nature.

How to Eliminate Misconceptions with Respect to Knowledge

The ultimate is not an object of
high knowledge or rationality.
It is realized by means of the blessing of the guru
and fortune ones with good karmic momentum.
That realization eliminates misconceptions with respect to knowledge.

The last of the five misconceptions has to do with the way that we think about learning and gaining knowledge. The great wisdom of the ultimate is not the object of logicians. We realize the true Dharma through the blessing of the guru. Those who have good qualities and the accumulation of merit are able to be freed from misconceptions with respect to wisdom.

Training in the Three Skills

Having explained the five misconceptions, we now move to the second of the three steps for developing your capacity: the training in the three skills. The three skills are divided into skill applied at the beginning of your meditation practice, skill applied when finishing the meditation session, and skill applied to sustain the experience of meditation practice. The next three verses explain these three sets of skills in greater detail.

At the Beginning: Skill at Commencing Meditation

Properly maintaining the crucial points of the body, look for the essence;
when active, look on the basis of the activity,
and when still, look on the basis of the stillness.
Rest on just that awareness of one's own nature without wandering
from the unfabricated fresh natural state just as it is.

First you need to train to develop skill in commencing meditation correctly. When meditating you should maintain the crucial points of the body that were explained earlier and then look at the essence of the mind. When the mind becomes active, and thoughts arrive, look directly at those thoughts without manipulating them or being manipulated by them. This is how one meditates on mental activity. When the mind remains calm, then with awareness of the essence of the mind, remain in such a state without wandering. This is how to use skill in commencing meditation on the nature of the mind.

In the Middle: Skill at Ceasing Meditation

Whatever your object of meditative equipoise,
do not concern yourself primarily with the duration.
Adjusting your meditative concentration and the crucial points of the body,
meditate in many short sessions, maintaining lucidity and intensity,
and you will not become resentful [of your practice] but will remain inspired.

Engaging in meditation sessions that are too long is one of the biggest mistakes that I see practitioners make. This is true of beginners and even long-time meditators. In mahāmudrā practice, the freshness of the meditation is more important than the duration of the meditation session. The maxim of valuing quality over quantity is applicable in this context. Long meditation sessions can lead to familiarization with dullness. Of course, if one is proficient at meditation and can maintain the vividness of their meditation practice for an extended period of time, then there is no problem with meditating for long stretches of time. The point is that when you practice meditative equipoise, your goal should not be guided by the duration of your meditation session. Instead, you should practice many short but fully focused sessions. You may change your focal object and move your body a little if you become tired or if your focus becomes dull. When you meditate in this way, it will not be stressful or difficult, and joy will arise whenever you practice.

In the End: Skill at Sustaining the Experience

> **Whichever of the three meditative experiences dawn—**
> **bliss, clarity, or nonconceptuality—**
> **since it is said that if you develop attachment to or pride about them**
> **you will lose realization for the sake of meditative experience,**
> **you should sustain [your meditation] in a state devoid of attachment to meditative experience.**

As your meditation practice develops and you are able to improve the quality of your meditation as you prolong the duration, then you will begin to have meditative experiences. We talk of three main types of meditative experiences: (1) experiences of bliss, (2) experiences of clarity, and (3) experiences of nonconceptuality. I will not describe these experiences in detail because the point here is that one should not develop attachment to these experiences and one should not develop pride upon attaining them. Whatever meditative experiences occur—whether bliss, clarity, or a nonconceptual state—if you try to hold on to them with attachment or allow pride about having achieved them to arise, then your meditative experience will be diminished, and your realization will be lost. Therefore, it is through giving up attachment to meditative experiences that one prolongs and cultivates one's practice.

Making Progress through Eliminating Deviations and Pitfalls

The third step for developing your capacity is making progress through eliminating deviations and pitfalls. Once you overcome these two main hurdles, then you will be able to make progress in developing and strengthening your practice. We will explain how to avoid deviations and then move onto avoiding pitfalls.

Eliminating Deviations

The next four verses explain four different types of deviation. The first is the deviation from emptiness as the nature of the object of knowledge.

Deviation from Emptiness as the Nature of the Object of Knowledge

> **Having determined the fundamental nature of things to be empty**
> **by means of the conventions involved in**
> **listening to and contemplating scripture and reasoning, one may think,**
> **"Since all things are empty, what reason is there to meditate?"**
> **Since this is posited by intellectual construction, it is incorrect.**

It is important to distinguish between genuine emptiness, which is unconstructed, and an understanding of emptiness that is conceptually constructed by the mind. You should not fall into the trap of believing that your mental construction captures genuine emptiness, because with such a concept, you are not really seeing things as they are; you are merely engaging in fabrication. When the mind contrives some idea of emptiness, this is not genuine emptiness.

There are two kinds of deviations from emptiness as the nature of the object of knowledge: the first is deviation since beginningless time and the second is present deviation. The first kind refers to how, despite the fact that everything has been empty since beginningless time, we have always contrived mistaken ideas about ourselves and the world with our misguided thoughts, due to fundamental ignorance about the nature of reality. The second kind of deviation refers to the idea that the emptiness you have understood through merely listening to the teachings is genuine emptiness; as explained, this kind of emptiness is merely a concept and not genuine emptiness.

Deviation from Emptiness as the Seal

The "deviation from emptiness as the seal"
refers to holding that all things are not empty,
but that they become empty by articulating the śūnyatā mantra, etc.
It is also not correct to meditate in this way.

The deviation from emptiness as the seal is the mistaken understanding of emptiness as something that is newly "colored" onto things. All the things we see around us already have emptiness as their nature. They have always been marked by the "seal" of emptiness. If you do not believe that they are empty but think that they are somehow *made* empty through uttering mantras like *om svabhāva śuddha sarva dharma svabhāva śuddho 'ham*, this is incorrect and amounts to a deviation from correct practice.

Deviation from Emptiness as the Antidote

> **The "deviation from emptiness as the antidote"**
> **refers to engaging in meditative equipoise thinking,**
> **"When thoughts such as the three poisons arise,**
> **I will destroy them with emptiness." This is flawed.**

Deviation from emptiness as the antidote involves regarding emptiness as a remedy that you must apply in order to eradicate defilements. This misguided approach involves taking ordinary thoughts as a target to be eradicated, and then recruiting emptiness from somewhere and using it as a tool to eradicate these thoughts, so as to end up at some other mental space. This amounts to looking for the profound somewhere else. Instead, you should simply look directly at ordinary thought itself. When a thought arises, look at the thought itself; this is where you are to practice. The essence of the thought itself is the dharmakāya.

Deviation from Emptiness as the Path

> **The "deviation from emptiness as the path"**
> **refers to thinking, "While the path and the result are nondual in terms of emptiness,**
> **I practice the path now by meditating on emptiness,**
> **and later I will obtain the result." This is incorrect.**

Deviation from emptiness as the path involves thinking, "I am using emptiness as the path to attain buddhahood," without the understanding that, ultimately, there is no path and no result.

In the Zurmang Whispered Tradition, the four deviations are summarized as follows:

1. Deviation from emptiness as the nature of the object of knowledge: This is imagining that we conceptually understand the

truth or essence of how everything abides. You should abandon such thoughts.

2. Deviation from emptiness as the seal: This involves believing that you have brought emptiness into being by means of mantras, etc., and that your mind has made emptiness, which is not the beginningless essence of things. You should abandon such fabrications and remain in the nature, trying to nurture ordinary mind.
3. Deviation from emptiness as the antidote: This involves thinking that all defilements are actually eradicated by the antidote of emptiness. You should abandon such dualistic ways of thinking and look at the thought itself. That will eradicate such a wrong view.
4. Deviation from emptiness as the path: This involves thinking that only emptiness is the path, without understanding the method aspect of the path. Seeing the union of saṃsāra and nirvāṇa will help you to overcome such a mistaken idea.

Making Progress by Avoiding Pitfalls to Meditation

Having covered the deviations, which are the wrong paths that one can stray down in meditation practice, we now turn to making progress by avoiding pitfalls to meditation. The text gives seventeen pitfalls to avoid.

As for the method for making progress by avoiding pitfalls, seventeen points will be explained in sequence:

1. From among the three of bliss, luminosity, and nonconceptuality,
as for the meditative experience of bliss,
intellectually examining bliss in general
without distinguishing between contaminated and uncontaminated bliss [is the first pitfall].

2. If you become completely attached [to that bliss] while meditating on it,
you will stray into the desire realm.
3. Likewise, if you are attached to the meditative experience of luminosity, you will stray into the form realm.
4. If you are attached to nonconceptuality,
you will be born in the formless realm.

As you progress in meditation, you will begin to have experiences such as bliss, luminosity, and nonduality. These experiences can actually become the basis for falling from the correct manner of practice. It is said that through becoming attached to these types of meditative experiences, one can be reborn in different realms. For example, if you become attached to the meditative experience of bliss, you will be reborn in one of the different regions of the desire realm, though not the ten lower realms. If you become attached to the meditative experience of luminosity, then there is the danger that you will be reborn in one of the seventeen abodes in the form realm. Similarly, if you become attached to the meditative experience of nonconceptuality, there is the danger of taking rebirth in one of the four formless realms. All of these kinds of rebirth will only delay your progress on the path to enlightenment and perpetuate your experience of cycling in saṃsāra.

5. Moreover, if you become completely attached to the discerning analysis
that "all phenomena are like space,"
you will be born in the sphere of limitless space.
6. Due to holding to the thought that "phenomena are [in fact] the mind,"
you will stray into the sphere of limitless consciousness.
7. If you become attached to the thought that nothing is established,
then you will stray in the sphere of nothingness.

8. If you become attached to the thought that there is neither existence nor nonexistence,
then you will be reborn in the sphere of neither discernment nor nondiscernment.

If you become attached to the analysis of all phenomena as space-like insofar as they have no color, no shape, no end, no center, etc., then you will be reborn in the first of the four states in the formless realm: the sphere of limitless space. If you grasp to the thought that the Buddha said that the entirety of the three realms is merely in the nature of mind, then you will be reborn in the second of the four states in the formless realm: the sphere of limitless consciousness. If you become attached to the thought that nothing really exists, then you will be reborn in the third of the four states in the formless realm: the sphere of nothingness. And if you become attached to the thought that there is neither existence nor nonexistence, then you will be reborn in the fourth of the four states in the formless realm: the sphere of neither discernment nor nondiscernment.

9. Thus, be free from desire and attachment
for the meditative experiences of bliss, luminosity, and nonconceptuality,
all [these pitfalls] will be avoided
by seeing the true face of the natural state.

10. Since it is by attachment to emptiness while lacking method,
that one strays into the lower way,
the method for eliminating this [pitfall] is to meditate
on love, compassion, and bodhicitta.

If you do not employ the method aspect of the practice, like developing love, compassion, and bodhicitta, and instead develop attachment to emptiness, then there is the danger that you will become concerned solely with personal liberation rather than benefiting all sentient beings. In order to avoid this pitfall, you should focus on developing love, compassion, and bodhicitta.

There are two types of bodhicitta: relative bodhicitta and ultimate bodhicitta. "Relative bodhicitta" refers to the mind that wishes to achieve complete enlightenment for the purpose of helping all beings. "Ultimate bodhicitta" refers to the realization of emptiness. When we talk about relative bodhicitta, we can further divide this into two types of activities: (1) aspiring bodhicitta and (2) engaging bodhicitta.

"Aspiring bodhicitta" refers to the act of wishing to be able to benefit all sentient beings. This is like how, when we are unable to give financial support to someone who needs it, we might hope that the next time someone needs our help, we will be in a better financial position to assist them. Aspiring bodhicitta involves the practice of generating good thoughts. We train in the practice of bodhicitta by giving selfless and unconditional love and compassion to others. As with any practice, there are different levels of training, but through constant practice, we will be able to perfect it.

Once we have the habit of generating these types of good thoughts, we can then take the next step and practice engaging bodhicitta; this is when we are wholeheartedly engaged in helping someone with the correct motivation. To begin this practice, we do not need to, for example, give away a huge amount of money. We can start with more comfortable acts like giving away one dollar.

Of course, our help should not be restricted to financial assistance. I'm just using this as an example because it is easy to understand. Another way that we can help others is by giving our time. The difference between aspiring and engaging bodhicitta is like the difference between wishing to go on a journey and actually taking the journey.

Generally, we begin by training first in relative bodhicitta. We should not, however, be content to direct our efforts at merely the relative level of practice. Once we are familiar with these types of relative bodhicitta, we can go further to the practice of ultimate bodhicitta, the understanding of emptiness. It is important that we try our best to emulate the buddhas by freeing ourselves from grasping to the three notions of agent, object, and action. When we practice positive actions such as generosity, we accumulate merit, and this will indeed bring about happiness in the future. However, this type of happiness is only temporary. But when we practice positive actions with ultimate bodhicitta, understanding the emptiness of the agent, object, and action, this will create the kind of merit that is the source of complete enlightenment. The practice of bodhicitta qualifies us as Mahāyāna practitioners. Love and compassion are the key to everything.

11. With method, you will make progress in knowledge.
12. With knowledge, you will make progress in method.
13. With the union of those two,
progress in one helps you make progress in the other.

Method, or skillful means, actually enables you to progress in your knowledge, or wisdom of emptiness. Conversely, the wisdom that understands the emptiness of the three spheres (i.e., oneself, one's action, and the object or recipient of one's actions) will enable you to utilize method as part of the uncontaminated path. With the union of skillful means and wisdom, these two aspects of the path are mutually reinforcing, which is why they are often referred to as the two wings of a bird, both essential for flight. With knowledge of emptiness alone, there is the danger of falling into the lower vehicle, and with method alone, one will not be able to traverse the uncontaminated path. So, the development of each helps you to make progress in the other.

14. Developing vipaśyanā advances śamatha.
15. Developing śamatha also advances vipaśyanā.

Without vipaśyanā, the practice of śamatha alone is a worldly practice, but the moment that vipaśyanā arises, śamatha becomes a part of the path to liberation. When vipaśyanā is born in you, it makes śamatha more profound. Without śamatha, vipaśyanā is inflexible like an old man's body, and one cannot attain any of the *siddhis*, the various attainments and capacities that arise as a result of becoming adept in meditation. The more that you practice śamatha, the better and more powerful your vipaśyanā will become. In this way, śamatha and vipaśyanā are mutually beneficial.

16. With respect to both śamatha and vipaśyanā,
at the level of single-pointedness, developing meditative experience
advances meditative experience.
Similarly, at the level of freedom from proliferation,
developing meditative experience advances realization.
At the level of one taste, developing realization
advances realization.
By transforming all ordinary actions of the three doors
without exception into a variety of virtues,
you will make progress at [transforming] the ordinary into excellent qualities.

In general, as soon as you learn something, you shouldn't just set it aside. Rather, you should continue to strive to perfect your understanding. It is only then that your learning will become the cause for deepening your understanding. Similarly, once you gain some meditative experience, continue to practice with that experience vigorously. Making effort with whatever meditative experience you have developed enables you to make further progress in your meditative experience, making it stronger, deeper, and closer to realization. So, you must make effort at maintaining your meditative experience once it arises not only in order to make progress in it, but most importantly in order to create the conditions for your meditative experience to transform into realization.

Likewise, once you have attained the realization of the first *bhūmi*, the path of seeing, as you progress from there through the paths of habituation and no more learning, your prior realizations will help you to progress in attaining further, deeper realizations.

17. Looking at the true face of faults, such as mental afflictions, suffering, and obstacles,
without discarding or adopting,
by taking bad omens to be auspicious, you will make progress.

Generally, when we have defilements, we try to overcome them and acquire positive qualities, knowledge, etc. But here, the instruction is to go beyond this way of thinking. Rather than trying to abandon all afflictions, suffering, and so forth, or trying to adopt any antidotes, you should simply look through, directly at the thought, at the face of the natural state. When you look in such a manner, you are able to make progress in terms of the practice of sameness, or suchness.

Making Progress by Crossing the Three Dangerous Passes

The last section on developing your capacity explains how to make progress by crossing the three "dangerous passages." The next three verses take us through three different types of dangerous passages.

Emptiness Arising as One's Enemy

When you analyze and look at the essence of mind,
having seen that nothing whatsoever is established,
you may fail to apprehend that which is to be rejected and its antidote,
thinking, "Since all phenomena are merely emptiness,
virtue and vice, cause and effect, and so on, are also not established."
This is known as "deluded chatter";
it is emptiness arising as one's enemy
and should be rejected like poison.

Emptiness arising as an enemy is the first dangerous passage. Of course, emptiness does not really do anything to hurt us. What is meant here is that you mistake emptiness for a form of nihilism and then believe that emptiness invalidates the law of natural cause and effect, and vice and virtue. This is why Maitreya Buddha said, "One who claims to believe in emptiness is more dangerous than one who believes in 'I'." Similarly, Master Śāntideva said that a realist is just like an animal who mistakenly sees things as truly existent, but a nihilist is the most dangerous, since it is this kind of wrong view that leads to ethical nihilism, which disregards moral virtue and vice. The view that because ultimately everything is empty, there is nothing to be abandoned or cultivated, is wrong and is a dangerous view.

Compassion Arising as One's Enemy

Once you have acquired a little bliss of meditative concentration,
you may think, "I will liberate sentient beings who do not have that."
Then, having given up the practice of meditative concentration,
you may exert yourself at various acts of virtue
and conceive of them to be truly existent;
this is known as "compassion arising as one's enemy."
In a state inseparable from the arising of compassion,
strive to sustain your stainless realization.

There is a danger that by seeing so much suffering in the world and seeing how urgently others need our help, that we believe we ought to abandon our spiritual practice and dive into the service of people's immediate material needs. This certainly is a noble mindset, but it also has an element of short-term thinking. We need to maintain our spiritual practice as we help others. Actually, seeing how urgently others need our help should fire up our urgency for striving to make progress in our practice. Through progress in spiritual practice we become much more effective at helping others, and the ultimate realization of enlightenment will enable you to help guide others not merely to temporary quick fixes for their suffering but to the state of the permanent cessation of all forms of suffering that is acquired upon liberation.

This is why the yogis of the past advised us to never give up our practice of meditative concentration. You should make sure that whatever realization of compassion that you have gained is not polluted by wrong views. Don't allow yourself to wander following internal or external distractions. Instead, you should practice in an isolated place and make real progress in your spiritual practice.

Cause and Result Arising as One's Enemy

If, thinking, "In order to realize the profound nature of reality,
I must become learned in all fields of knowledge,"
you undertake the study of grammar, epistemology, and so forth,
and give up the practice of śamatha and vipaśyanā,
this is known as "the thought of cause and effect arising as one's enemy";
it is incorrect.
Thus, by meditating single-pointedly on the profound meaning,
you will obtain the undeluded stainless knowledge of
all phenomenal appearances in saṃsāra and nirvāṇa.

You might mistakenly believe that in order to realize the essence of mind, you must become learned in all fields of knowledge, such as the five traditional branches of learning: grammar, logic, craftsmanship, medicine, and religion. We have to be intelligent about how we spend our time. If, for example, you start learning Tibetan so that you can better understand the teachings, then this is wonderful, but if at the same time you do so at the expense of actual meditation practice, then this is like thinking you are making progress when you are actually working against your own goals. You should practice the union of wisdom and compassion and overcome confusion with respect to saṃsāra and nirvāṇa. By realizing the profound meaning of the ultimate, everything will be realized.

7. HOW TO ELIMINATE OBSTACLES

NEXT, THE TEXT MOVES from advice on how to develop one's capacity to instructions for how to eliminate obstacles to successful practice. A yogi needs to know how to work with three different types of obstacles: sickness, demonic interferences, and specific obstacles related to meditative concentration. A skillful practitioner can actually bring these obstacles into the path and utilize them as the support for their practice. The next few verses explain how to work with illness in your meditation practice.

Eliminating Obstacles of Sickness

Through primarily practicing śamatha, wind diseases are eliminated.
Through practicing vipaśyanā, diseases of phlegm and bile are eliminated.
Moreover, diseases related to heat and cold are gradually eliminated
by practicing both śamatha and vipaśyanā.

Likewise, examine the essence of whatever sickness you have:

its shape, its source, and where it goes.
In particular, make special effort at sending and taking (*tonglen*).

Alternatively: The nonarising of illness is the dharmakāya.
Its nonabiding is the saṃbhogakāya. Its nonceasing is the nirmāṇakāya.
Its empty nature is the svabhāvakāya.
Taking [illness] to be the play of the four kāyas, look at its true face.

Through examining the essence of sickness itself, you will arrive at emptiness. When you analyze where this sickness arises from, where it abides, and where it goes, you see the nature of sickness. Then it is said that you will be able to overcome all kinds of illness.

The practice of vipaśyanā is said to balance the elements of the subtle body in such a way that it helps with illnesses associated with phlegm, which is associated with the elements of earth and water. It is also said that śamatha practice balances the elements of the subtle body in such a way that it helps with illness associated with wind. Vipaśyanā and śamatha are said to help with illnesses that are related to heat and cold. Śamatha is like the moon, a cool breeze, or cool water, and helps cure diseases related to heat. Vipaśyanā is said to be like the sun, whose rays dry up pools of water and can help cure diseases related to dampness.

Another strategy for overcoming illness is to contemplate how the nature of sickness relates to the four kāyas: Like the dharmakāya, illness is unarisen. Like the saṃbhogakāya, illness does not abide. Like the nirmāṇakāya, illness does not cease. And because illness is empty of intrinsic nature, it is the svabhāvakāya. If we look directly at the nature of illness, it is said that we can eliminate it. Whatever we might think about these advices, it is certain that we can use problems such as illness as a powerful support for our spiritual practice.

Eliminating Demonic Obstacles

Likewise, as for the way to eliminate demonic obstacles:
The appearance of demons is the magical play of the mind.
Take the mind itself to be the four kāyas
and eliminate demons too by means of
taking them into the path of the four kāyas.

Whatever you are seeing as external evil spirits, ghosts, etc., are all fabrications of the mind. You must see that everything is in the nature of mind, and that mind itself is luminous and yet empty. Without having attachment or ego-clinging, see the mind as the four kāyas. When you think in this way, you will be able to overcome all demonic obstacles.

Eliminating Obstacles to Meditative Concentration

In general, the method for eliminating the faults
of dullness and agitation is as previously explained.
Now, to eliminate [these] by means of guru yoga:

When you [experience] dullness, [visualize] Guru
Amitābha on your crown;
the lineage gurus and so forth dissolve into him,
and by virtue of invoking him with devotion,
light rays emanate and dissolve into you,
whereupon the causes for dullness are completely purified.
The guru melts into light and dissolves into you,
whereby your body transforms into a ball of light,
and the entire pure realm is made manifest,
whereupon it dissolves into space.
Rest the mind lucidly, with intensified awareness.

As discussed earlier, all the obstacles to meditative concentration can be summarized into two: dullness and agitation. The common way for dealing with the meditative obstacles of dullness and agitation was explained above. Here is presented a more powerful method of eliminating these obstacles to meditative concentration through the practice of guru yoga.

When dullness arises, visualize on your crown your guru in the form of Amitābha Buddha, red in color. All the lineage gurus, buddhas, and bodhisattvas dissolve into your guru. Arouse a sense of devotion and make aspirational prayers. From the body of the guru, light radiates and dissolves into you, and all forms of dullness are immediately purified. The guru dissolves into light, revealing to you the entire pure land. The light rays emanate out into space, and your mind becomes extremely sharp and focused.

> **If you [experience] agitation, visualize guru Vajrasattva, blue in color,**
> **In the middle of a four-petaled lotus at your heart;**
> **on the four petals are Vairocana, and so forth, the same in color,**
> **surrounded by the vīras, ḍākinīs, and so forth belonging to their families.**
> **Visualize blue light emanating from their hearts**
> **piercing the guru, and light rays spread in all directions.**
> **Eliminate [agitation] by resting in equipoise in the state of mahāmudrā.**

When agitation arises, visualize your guru as Vajrasattva, blue in color, sitting on a four-petaled lotus at your heart. Vajrasattva in the center is surrounded by the buddhas of the four other buddha families: Vairocana in the east, Ratnasambhava in the south, Amitābha in the west, and Amoghasiddhi in the north. Each is surrounded by vīras, ḍākinīs, etc., belonging to his family and in the respective color. Blue light radiates from their hearts and pierces the central guru. The light becomes like a tent. Remain in mahāmudrā.

Moreover, whichever of dullness or agitation occurs, rest naturally
on its essence without wandering, without meditating, without contrivance.

Whenever dullness or agitation arises, you can also look directly at the mind without wandering, without meditating, and without fabricating anything. Simply rest the mind naturally.

You should apply the appropriate antidotes as discussed earlier, but here is presented the special method of guru yoga. If you are lacking in bliss in your body, then visualize your guru as Amitabha Buddha. If you are lacking in luminosity, then visualize your guru as Akṣobhya. If you are lacking in nondiscursiveness, and are distracted, then visualize your guru as Vairocana. With this method, you will experience fewer obstacles and will be able to progress in your practice.

8. HOW TO TRAVERSE THE PATH

HAVING COVERED HOW to realize one's potential and how to deal with obstacles, we now move on to how one progresses on the spiritual path. We will be using two frameworks to understand the yogi's development on the path: the four yogas and the twelve stages. First, we will discuss how to traverse higher and higher on the path by way of the four yogas, and then by way of the twelve stages.

Teaching How to Traverse Higher and Higher on the Path by Way of the Four Yogas

The four yogas are an important part of the mahāmudrā teachings. The four yogas are (1) single-pointedness, (2) freedom from fabrication, (3) one taste, and (4) nonmeditation. The twelve stages are actually arrived at by dividing each of the four yogas into three substages: lesser, middling, and superior.

I should emphasize right at the beginning that, in some sense, mahāmudrā does not depend on exerting effort to traverse a path. As Shang Rinpoche said, "Mahāmudrā itself is a single stride. Fools who delineate stages and paths are deluded." It is true that mahāmudrā is one realization, and if you try to elaborate it in terms of grounds and paths, then this is a delusion. However, generally speaking, in order to bring a practitioner to the right path, different skillful means are taught, based on the capacity of the disciple—for instance, whether they are a simultaneist, a bypasser, or a gradualist. So, in the mahāmudrā tradition, the four yogas can be used to describe how to traverse the Buddhist path from the very beginning until the achievement of enlightenment.

The First Yoga: Single-Pointedness

> **Firstly, as for the yoga of single-pointedness:**
> **awareness of the true nature of mind,**
> **remains clearly and lucidly in the state**
> **of space-like unceasing luminosity and emptiness, without center or limit.**
>
> **Dividing that into lesser, middling, and superior:**
> **The lesser is seeing the essence of bliss and luminosity.**
> **The middling is attaining mastery in meditative concentration.**
> **The superior is meditative experience becoming constant.**

The first of the four yogas, single-pointedness, is the stage of practice when a practitioner has some level of stabilization of their meditative experience in relation to the nature of their mind. Awareness is not blurred but completely clear. At this time, the meditative experiences of bliss, luminosity, and nonconceptuality will arise.

There are three levels of single-pointedness, which are related to the level of familiarity with these experiences of bliss, luminosity, and nonconceptuality. Single-pointedness for those of the lower level involves the meditative experience that the mind is blissful, luminous, and empty. Whenever a thought arises, the instruction is to simply leave things as they are, and one will see that mental activity will simply dissolve. The thoughts will just dissipate like a cloud disappearing into the sky, and these three meditative experiences of bliss, clarity, and nonconceptuality will dawn. Everything that arises is experienced as bliss, luminosity, and nonconceptuality once all ordinary thoughts have ceased. At that time, one has attained the lesser level of single-pointedness; however, one has not mastered this technique.

Sometimes when you meditate, you may have these experiences of bliss, luminosity, and nonconceptuality, and then at other times, these experiences may not arise. At this stage, you only have meditative experience, not realization. This meditative experience of single-pointedness is like the first day after a new moon, where you only see a sliver of the moon, but cannot see the whole moon. You have the beginning of wisdom and are just starting out on the path. You must continue with your practice of meditation.

As for single-pointedness for those of the middling level, even when you are not meditating, these meditative experiences of bliss, luminosity, and nonconceptuality will arise automatically. At this stage then, even post-meditation activities can become the path of meditation, and when you do meditate, your meditations become more stable. Earlier, thoughts would arise, but now thoughts become fewer and fewer, and whatever arises becomes the path of meditation. It is said all kinds of miraculous powers can be attained at this stage.

As for single-pointedness for those of the higher level, earlier there was a distinction between meditative equipoise and post-meditation. At this point, whether one is engaged in any of the four kinds of conduct, the three kinds of meditative experience are fully present at all times. At this stage of superior single-pointedness, one has reached the state where meditative experience is constantly present.

The Second Yoga: Freedom from Fabrication

Freedom from fabrication is the realization that the mind itself is ungrounded.
Having become liberated from fabrications
concerning the arising, ceasing, and abiding
of all dualistic phenomena,

and from grasping at characteristics,
cut superimpositions concerning unborn emptiness.

All meditative experiences are without a place to reside; all are empty. When you realize the true essence of mind, the true essence of rigpa, then like removing the husk of a grain, you will discover what is truly inside, like a treasure. At this time, you become truly realized. This is called freedom from proliferation.

The freedom from fabrication is the realization that the mind itself is free of a fixed foundation. When you remain meditating single-pointedly without attachment, and do not rely on effort, whether the mind is resting or moving, the simultaneously born wisdom dawns. At that time, you will truly understand that everything is empty, or free from fabrication.

The lesser [level] is the realization that one's mind is unarisen.
The middling is freedom from the fundamental root
of grasping at appearances and grasping at emptiness.
The superior is cutting the superimpositions that fabricate all phenomena.

During the time of lesser freedom from fabrication, you realize the essence of your mind as free from arising and ceasing. During the time of middling freedom from fabrication, you experience that there is no foundation at all, and all things simply dissolve. During the time of superior freedom from fabrication, you have confidence that whatever is seen is in the nature of mind, and that mind itself is empty, and everything is like space.

The Third Yoga: One Taste

The yoga of one taste is the mixing of appearances and mind.
All phenomenal appearances of saṃsāra and nirvāṇa,

are equal in terms of the natural state,
neither free nor unfree from the fabrication of arising and ceasing,
neither empty nor nonempty,
neither negated nor established, neither discarded nor adopted.

The lesser [level] is the mixing into one equal taste
of all phenomena included in both [saṃsāra and nirvāṇa].
The middling is when appearance and mind are like water poured into water.
The superior is when all phenomena are pacified in the state of equality.

Nothing is unique or different from anything else in terms of its essence, just like an apple that has the same taste wherever you bite it. In terms of essence, all appearances are one.

The higher you go through the levels of one taste, your meditative experience becomes deeper, stronger, and more stable, and you realize that all appearances in saṃsāra and nirvāṇa are equal in being unborn. By the time you arrive at the middling level, appearance and mind become completely nondifferentiable, like water poured into water. Finally, at the superior level, whatever appears, you will never reify it, being completely pacified within the state of the equality of all dharmas. The realization of nonthought will be continually present, day and night.

The Fourth Yoga: Nonmeditation

Nonmeditation is the purification of one's earlier meditative experiences
or the utter cessation of the intellectual mind.
That has lesser, middling, and superior levels:
The lesser is when there is no object of meditation or meditator.

The middling is when you have taken hold of the natural place of spontaneity.
The superior is when, having mixed the mother and son clear light,
and having become diffused into the expanse of wisdom, the dharmadhātu,
one accomplishes the two aims and attains complete enlightenment.

Earlier, mindfulness was used as a tool to assist with your meditation, but when you reach the state of lesser nonmeditation, mindfulness is no longer required, and everything becomes meditation. There is no longer the thought of objects of meditation, the action of meditation, or the meditator. All states are simply meditation.

Middling nonmeditation occurs after you have been able to reach spontaneity and you are able to hold your position of spontaneity. Your level of realization then becomes cemented. You will realize that saṃsāra and nirvāṇa are beginninglessly self-arisen; no one created any of this.

When you reach nonmeditation of the highest capacity, all consciousness will transform into wisdom, and all obstacles to knowledge will be eliminated. The mother-like luminosity and son-like luminosity will become inseparable. During this time, one will attain liberation, and there will be no distinction between meditation and post-meditation. It is at this stage that you acquire the dharmakāya and svabhāvakāya for the sake of oneself and the saṃbhogakāya and nirmāṇakāya for the sake of others.

The Twelve Stages: Dividing Each of the Four Yogas into the Three of Lesser, Middling, and Superior

If one were to correspond the twelve yogas
to the grounds and paths according to the perfection of wisdom:

Lesser single-pointedness is the path of accumulation.
Middling is the heat and peak levels of the path of preparation.
Superior single-pointedness is the forbearance and supreme attribute levels of the path of preparation.

Lesser freedom from fabrication is the path of seeing, the first bodhisattva level.
Middling is from the second to the fifth bodhisattva levels.
At the time of the superior, the sixth bodhisattva level is attained.

Through the realization of lesser one taste, one [reaches] the seventh bodhisattva level.
Middling is the eighth bodhisattva level.
Superior one taste corresponds to the ninth bodhisattva level.

Lesser nonmeditation corresponds to the tenth bodhisattva level.
Middling is the limit of the continuum.
Superior is the completion of the path, corresponding to the eleventh bodhisattva level.

The lesser level of single-pointedness is part of the path of accumulation. The middling level of single-pointedness corresponds to the heat and peak levels, which are the first two levels of the path of preparation. Here, you may have the meditative experience of luminosity and emptiness if you have mindfulness, but if mindfulness is not thoroughly present, then the experience of luminosity and emptiness will not be continuously present. Before you experience the unfabricated blaze of wisdom of the path of seeing, you reach the heat level of the path of preparation, and an experience close to the clarity and appearance of dharmatā will arise. At this point, your experience will begin to become perfected, and your realization is about to dawn. The superior level of the yoga of single-pointedness corresponds to the third and fourth levels of the path of preparation, the forbearance and supreme attribute levels. Here, meditative experience will be continuously present, and all thoughts will dissolve into your meditative experience. Day and night, you will have the meditative experience of space-like luminosity and emptiness, and you will feel that you have reached nonmeditation, though you have not yet attained that state.

Having stabilized and habituated your experience of the clarity of dharmatā, you then move closer to the realization of the freedom from fabrication of the path of seeing, which is beyond worldly paths. Maintain your practice conjoined with devotion, and during this time, whatever arises, do not grasp onto it or engage in conceptual fabrication. Simply remain in such a state. The meditative experience of single-pointedness will become perfect and the meditative experience of freedom from fabrication will arise. As soon as it has arisen, you will have attained the path of seeing, which corresponds to the lesser level of the yoga of the freedom from fabrication. When you realize that all dharmas are beyond arising, ceasing, or abiding, this realization becomes the foundation for all knowledge to be acquired. At that moment, you become so joyful, and thus, this path, the first bodhisattva level, or bhūmi, is called the "Joyous."

Having realized that all phenomena are free from the clouds of fabrication and defilements of what is to be abandoned by the path of meditation, you have reached the second bodhisattva level, which is called the "Stainless." This stage corresponds to the start of the middling level of freedom from fabrication. Mind that never arises, abides, or ceases is not something new but has been there throughout time without beginning. This realization has always been present, and with the blessing of the light of the guru, it has finally been recognized and actualized. Therefore, the third bodhisattva level is called the "Luminous." When you attain the realization of the freedom from foundation, the knowledge of the buddhas will begin to brilliantly arise, enabling you to fulfill the aims of sentient beings and carry out beneficial activities on their behalf. For this reason, the fourth bodhisattva level is called the "Radiant." When you realize the union of emptiness and compassion, all the subtle habitual tendencies will be totally purified, and for this reason, the fifth bodhisattva level is called the "Difficult to Conquer."

The superior level of freedom from fabrication begins with the attainment of the sixth bodhisattva level. At this point, you will manifestly realize the nonexistence of saṃsāra and nirvāṇa. The sixth bodhisattva level is thus called the "Manifest."

Now you will begin to feel that you and others are one, mixed together inseparably like water poured into water. When such a realization arises in your mental continuum, you will also have the realization of union of saṃsāra and nirvāṇa. This will help you to overcome attachment to the emptiness of the Śrāvakayāna and Pratyekabuddhayāna, and you will distance yourself from these lesser vehicles. This is the attainment of the lesser division of the yoga of one taste, which corresponds to the seventh bodhisattva level, the "Gone Afar."

Then, upon attaining the middling level of the yoga of one taste, dualism will be totally eradicated, and everything will appear in the form of the ultimate truth, the natural state. This corresponds to the eighth bodhisattva level. Since at this point you will never be able to be moved from the state that is free from dualistic perception, the eighth bodhisattva level is called the "Unshakable."

At the superior level of the yoga of one taste, whatever appears in the post-meditation period will be seen as an unreal illusion. When such a realization dawns and is habituated, you will gain the profound knowledge arisen from meditation, such as the four types of wisdom, and you will have attained the ninth bodhisattva level, which is accordingly called "Good Intelligence."

Upon reaching the lesser level of nonmeditation, you will realize that there is no object of meditation or act of meditation. All the knowledge of a buddha will begin to appear like clouds gathering in the sky. This is the tenth bodhisattva level, called "Cloud of Dharma."

When you reach the middling level of nonmeditation, you have a tight hold on the place of self-arisen spontaneity, and at this time, the subtlest obstacles to knowledge will be thoroughly eradicated. At this time too, you will reach the final meditation of the "Special Path of the Limit of the Continuum," which is the final path immediately before buddhahood. This corresponds to the vajra-like samādhi of the moment before enlightenment.

Finally, you will realize the essence of nonthought, whereupon all subtle defilements of negative tendencies become purified, and all the knowledge of the Buddha is thoroughly attained. At this point the mother-like luminosity and son-like luminosity will merge, and the superior level of nonmeditation is attained. This corresponds to the attainment of buddhahood, which is the eleventh bodhisattva level.

9. HOW TO ACTUALIZE THE RESULT

In that way, once the twelve yogas have progressively arisen
in one's mental continuum and nonmeditation is accomplished,
the two obscurations and the entirety of karmic imprints will be eradicated
and the fruition of the wisdom of the two knowledges will be completed.
Though not moving from the dharmakāya for one's own sake,
for the sake of others, the rūpakāya will enact the benefit of beings
until saṃsāra is empty,
without conceptual thought, effort, striving, or proliferations,
with continuous enlightened activity
and the spontaneous presence of the pervasive nature.

Through this profound practice it is possible to overcome the two obscurations, the afflictive obscurations and the knowledge obscurations, and to thereby reach complete enlightenment. Complete enlightenment consists of the union of the dharmakāya and rūpakāya. The dharmakāya consists of the jñānadharmakāya and svabhāvakāya. The jñānadharmakāya corresponds to luminosity while the svabhāvakāya corresponds to emptiness. The rūpakāya consists of the saṃbhogakāya and the nirmāṇakāya. The saṃbhogakāya acts for the benefit of bodhisattvas on the tenth bhūmi, while the nirmāṇakāya acts for the benefit of all sentient beings. In this way, as a buddha, one will benefit sentient beings continuously, according to their different needs and capacities.

Dedication

Consequently, it is said:

By virtue of this effort and the merit acquired here,
in this life and in all lives to come,
may I properly remain in a state of renunciation of saṃsāra,
and may I never transgress even the slightest of the fundamental precepts!

May I never forget even in my dreams the two bodhicittas that benefit others,
and using the four means for gathering disciples
and the practice of the six perfections,
may I establish all beings in bliss!

May I cherish qualified spiritual guides
as I do my own life,
and pleasing them with all kinds of service,
may I always have faith and maintain my samaya.

In dependence on the power of this [virtue], with respect to the entire tripiṭaka—
the pratimokṣa, bodhisattva, and Mantrayāna of the knowledge holders—

for my own sake, may I listen, contemplate, and meditate.
For the sake of others, may I teach, debate, and compose treatises.
For both myself and others, may I become learned, disciplined, and good hearted.
For the sake of the teachings, may I uphold, protect, and propagate them.
May all this be fully accomplished!

Having gained realization in accordance
with the treatises on the irreversible definitive meaning,
and particularly the natural state of mahāmudrā,
may I become the one to spread it!

In summary, may I alone be able to establish
all beings without exception
filling the extent of space
in the state of complete and perfect buddhahood!

With the blessings of the triple gem
and the power of my pure superior intention,
and through the force of the profound emptiness and dependent origination,
may all these aspirations be achieved just so!

This text was requested by Nedo Kuchung Choktrul Rinpoche and Dilyak Lama Tsethar during their three-year retreat. With a pure intention to help others, Bokar Tulku Rinpoche composed this text at Rumtek Monastery.

Part IV: Translation

10. DETAILED OUTLINE OF THE ROOT TEXT

A Concise Commentary on the Ocean of Definitive Meaning: Easy-to-Implement Root Verses for Unlocking the Door to the Definitive Meaning

Part I: The Preliminaries

1 The common preliminaries

1.1 The difficulty of acquiring this life with its opportunities and resources

1.2 Death and impermanence

1.3 Karmic cause and effect

1.4 Faults of saṃsāra.

2 The uncommon preliminaries

2.1 Refuge and prostrations (Instructions for making one's mental continuum a suitable vessel, i.e., for developing the mind that goes for refuge, traveling the path to liberation in whatever one does)

2.2 Vajrasattva (Instructions for Vajrasattva meditation and recitation, which purifies negativities and obscurations)

2.3 Maṇḍala offering (Instructions for the mandala offering, which completes the two accumulations)

2.4 Guru yoga (Instructions for guru yoga, which enables one to quickly receive blessings)

3 The special preliminaries
3.1 The causal condition
3.2 The empowering condition
3.2.1 The lineage guru
3.2.2 The guru of the Sugata's speech
3.2.3 The guru using the symbols of appearances
3.2.4 The guru of ultimate dharmatā
3.3 The supporting condition
3.4 The immediately preceding condition

Part II: The Actual Practice

4 Śamatha
4.1 A general presentation of śamatha
4.1.1 Crucial points of the body
4.1.2 Crucial points of the mind
4.2 A detailed presentation of śamatha
4.2.1 Settling the mind that has not been settled
4.2.1.1 Concentrating with an object
4.2.1.1.1 Focusing on external objects
4.2.1.1.1.1 Concentrating on ordinary objects
4.2.1.1.1.2 Concentrating on extraordinary objects
4.2.1.1.2 Focusing on internal objects
4.2.1.2 Concentrating without an object
4.2.1.3 Concentrating on the breath
4.2.2 Stabilizing the mind that has been settled
4.2.2.1 Holding the mind
4.2.2.1.1 Holding the mind above
4.2.2.1.2 Holding the mind below
4.2.2.1.3 Holding the mind both above and below
4.2.2.2 Ninefold method for resting the mind

4.2.3 Enhancing the mind that has been stabilized.

5 Vipaśyanā
5.1 Looking at the nature of reality, the essence of mind
5.2 Cutting the fundamental root
5.3 Introduction by determining awareness to be empty
5.3.1 Introduction on the basis of movement
5.3.2 Introduction on the basis of appearance
5.3.2.1 Introducing appearance as the mind
5.3.2.2 Introducing mind itself as empty
5.3.2.3 Introducing emptiness as spontaneity
5.3.2.4 Introducing spontaneity as self-liberated

Part II: Conclusion

6 How to develop one's capacity and make progress
6.1 Making progress by dispelling the five misconceptions
6.1.1 How to eliminate misconceptions with respect to the object
6.1.2 How to eliminate misconceptions with respect to time
6.1.3 How to eliminate misconceptions with respect to the essence
6.1.4 How to eliminate misconceptions with respect to the nature
6.1.5 How to eliminate misconceptions with respect to knowledge
6.2 Training in the three skills
6.2.1 At the beginning: skill at commencing meditation
6.2.2 In the middle: skill at ceasing meditation
6.2.3 In the end: skill at sustaining the experience
6.3 Making progress through eliminating deviations and pitfalls
6.3.1 Eliminating deviations
6.3.1.1 Deviation from emptiness as the nature of the object of knowledge
6.3.1.2 Deviation from emptiness as the seal
6.3.1.3 Deviation from emptiness as the antidote
6.3.1.4 Deviation from emptiness as the path
6.3.2 Making progress by avoiding pitfalls to meditation
6.4 Making progress by crossing the three dangerous passes

6.4.1 Emptiness arising as one's enemy
6.4.2 Compassion arising as one's enemy
6.4.3 Cause and result arising as one's enemy

7 How to eliminate obstacles
7.1 Eliminating obstacles of sickness
7.2 Eliminating demonic obstacles
7.3 Eliminating obstacles to meditative concentration

8 How to traverse the path
8.1 Teaching how to traverse higher and higher on the path by way of the four yogas
8.1.1 The first yoga: single-pointedness
8.1.2 The second yoga: freedom from fabrication
8.1.3 The third yoga: one taste
8.1.4 The fourth yoga: nonmeditation
8.2 The twelve stages: dividing each of the four yogas into the three of lesser, middling, and superior

9 How to actualize the result
9.1 Dedication

11. TRANSLATION OF ROOT TEXT

The guru, the deity, and one's own mind,
being indivisible, are one in the natural state.
At all times, I prostrate and
wholeheartedly go for refuge to that.

With an intent to benefit those who wish to engage the Ocean of Definitive Meaning, *the guide to the co-emergent union of mahāmudrā, I set down here the outline of the text, and for the sake of easily understanding the stages of meditation related to it, I shall lay out root verses which summarize its meaning, and which is brief, clear, and suitable for recitation during meditation.*

Part I: The Preliminaries

1. The Common Preliminaries

The common preliminaries consist of meditating on four topics: (1) the difficulty of acquiring opportunities and resources, (2) death and impermanence, (3) karmic cause and effect, and (4) the faults of saṃsāra.

1.1 The Difficulty of Acquiring This Life with Its Opportunites and Resources

Namo gurubhyaḥ
In order to practice the excellent Dharma correctly one must abandon wandering.
The first object of meditation is the fact that this excellent foundation,
which is endowed with the eight opportunities and ten resources,
is difficult to acquire, and since it is extremely beneficial,
it is just like a wish-fulfilling jewel.

In particular, by relying on Vajrayāna,
this vajra body, which is endowed with the ṣix elements
for attaining enlightenment in a single lifetime, is even more rare.

Moreover, [this precious human rebirth] is difficult to acquire
in virtue of the three of cause, example, and number,
And even if it is acquired, it is extremely easy to die.
Thus, from now on, one should strive at meditating on the genuine, excellent Dharma.

1.2 Death and Impermanence

All conditioned phenomena—external and internal, the environment and beings—
are impermanent, even momentarily, in accordance with the four ends.

In particular, the lifespan of beings is
like a butter lamp in the midst of a windstorm,
and like a water bubble.
Indeed, I will certainly die;
the time of death is uncertain, yet death will come soon.
There are many conditions for death,
and though I may not want to, I will die nonetheless.
There is no one whatsoever who has been able to overcome death.

When I die, I will continuously experience unbearable suffering,
and at that time, there is no refuge apart from the excellent Dharma.
Therefore, I should control my mind, develop disillusionment,
and with a strong sense of urgency, throw myself into the practice of virtue.

1.3 Karmic Cause and Effect

After death, like a butter lamp whose oil is depleted,
I will have no power over where I am born.
Without any control, I will certainly follow my karma.
In general, all the variety of appearances of happiness and suffering
are said to be the results of virtuous and nonvirtuous karma.

Moreover, one should contemplate in detail how
due to engaging in the ten virtues, one will be reborn in the higher realms,
and due to engaging in the ten nonvirtues under the control of mental afflictions,
one will be reborn in the lower realms.

In short, the results of my own actions will never disappear,
but I will certainly experience them.
Therefore, I should strive at the proper way of
adopting virtue and discarding vice,
and investigate my own mental continuum.

1.4 Faults of Saṃsāra

Wherever one is born among the six classes of beings
within the three realms of saṃsāra,
One will be thoroughly and continuously
oppressed by the three kinds of suffering.
Moreover, one should contemplate how one will experience

these forms of suffering intensely and for a long time:
the suffering of heat and cold as a hell being,
the suffering of hunger and thirst as a hungry ghost,
the suffering of eating one another as an animal,
the suffering of birth, old age, sickness, and death, etc., as a human,
the suffering of quarrelling as a demigod,
and the suffering of dying and falling from the status of a god.

Even the slightest appearance
of pleasure or riches within saṃsāra
should be abandoned like poisoned food.
Now is the time to strive at the method for
definitely liberating oneself from saṃsāra, which is like a fire pit.

2. The Uncommon Preliminaries

2.1 Refuge and Prostrations

Therefore, apart from the three jewels,
there is no refuge that can protect me
from the suffering of existence.
Thus, I and all beings that fill the expanse of space go for refuge
and visualize as follows:

In the space in front of me is a wish-fulfilling tree with five
branches.
In the middle, sitting atop a lion throne, lotus, and moon
is my root guru, Lord Vajradhāra, clear and brilliant,
and complete with the major and minor marks.

Above that are the lineage gurus in tiers:
in front, on the right, behind, and on the left, respectively
sit the yidam, the Buddha, the Dharma, and the Sangha,
gathered like a heap of clouds.

I and all beings go for refuge until attaining complete enlightenment,
and develop supreme bodhicitta.
Finally, the objects of refuge melt into light and,
dissolving into my own three doors,
rest in the natural state.

2.2 Vajrasattva

I confess all negativities and downfalls accumulated from beginningless time,
by means of the four powers, and in particular,
I shall engage in the supreme power of applying the antidote,
undertaking the meditation and recitation of Vajrasattva:

Myself in ordinary form,
sitting atop my crown is Guru Vajrasattva, body white in color;
his right hand holds a five-pointed vajra at his heart;
his left hand holds a bell at his hip;
he is seated in the bodhisattva posture.

Appearing, yet essenceless, within his body, at his luminous heart,
atop a moon disk, is a *hūṃ* surrounded by the hundred syllable mantra.
From that a stream of nectar descends and enters through the aperture of Brahmā,
purifying all of one's negativities, obscurations, and defilements without exception.

Having recited [the mantra] again and again, Vajrasattva becomes pleased,
and grants confirmation with the words
"All your negativities and obscurations are purified!"
He melts into light and dissolves into me,
whereby I become indivisible with the three vajras.

2.3 Maṇḍala Offering

In reliance on the supreme method of offering a pure realm,
one should amass the two collections of merit and wisdom.
Visualize as follows:
The practice maṇḍala is made of precious substances,
unsullied by the stains of faults.

In front of oneself, properly visualize
a luminous celestial mansion, with completely perfect attributes,
in the middle of which are one's root and lineage gurus, surrounded in the four directions
by the yidam, Buddha, Dharma, and Sangha,
together with vīras, ḍākinīs, and wisdom protectors.
Visualize a maṇḍala offering adorned with billions [of universes],
including Mount Meru, the four continents, and four subcontinents.

Furthermore, visualize and offer everything that exists without exception—
the bodies, wealth, and collections of virtue,
belonging to oneself and all beings equal to the expanse of space.
By this power, may the two collections be fully completed.
The deities, being delighted, melt into light and dissolve into me,
and we become nondual.

2.4 Guru Yoga

The foundation of all good qualities,
and particularly the supreme method for realizing the ultimate, mahāmudrā,
is nothing other than the blessing of the glorious guru.

Thus, perform guru yoga as follows:
Visualizing myself as the yidam deity,

on my crown is my root guru, Lord Vajradhāra,
above whom sit the lineage gurus, one atop the other,
and surrounded by yidams, buddhas, bodhisattvas,
vīras, ḍākinīs, and wisdom protectors.

Through the power of making offerings and reciting prayers to them,
the surrounding retinue dissolves into the principal guru.
The principal guru then encompasses the nature of all objects of refuge.
Once more, I request the bestowal of empowerment,
and the four empowerments are received.

The four obscurations are purified, and the seeds for the four kāyas are planted.
Then, the guru, being delighted, melts into light,
and dissolves into me,
and I remain in the state of mahāmudrā.

3. The Special Preliminaries

There are four special preliminaries: (1) the causal condition, (2) the empowering condition, (3) the supporting condition, and (4) the immediately preceding condition.

3.1 The Causal Condition

Discipline the mind well, and having contemplated
renunciation and the desire for liberation,
cut off all attachments, and
simply remain as a renunciant in an isolated place,
without outer or inner wandering.

3.2 The Empowering Condition

3.2.1 The Lineage Guru

From Vajradhāra down to my root guru,
a stream of blessings, oral instructions, and so forth,
has passed down uninterruptedly, one-to-one,
in an authentic lineage until reaching my guru.

3.2.2 The Guru of the Sugata's Speech

Having given rise to conviction in all that the guru has taught,
by developing the experiential understanding
that it is in no way contradictory with the word of the Jina,
all scriptures will appear as instructions.

3.2.3 The Guru Using the Symbols of Appearances

Because [the guru] teaches the methods of the path
by means of symbols and examples
making use of all phenomena—the outer and inner objects
of saṃsāra and nirvāṇa, including the elements
and whatever has arisen from the elements—
all things are nothing other than the guru.

3.2.4 The Guru of Ultimate Dharmatā

Due to establishing the unmistaken realization,
which is the direct perception of the nature of one's own mind
in accordance with how it was introduced by the glorious guru,
one also realizes the nature of reality of all phenomena.

3.3 The Supporting Condition

One should take as the object of practice
the nature of mind, which is the primordial reality that is unaltered
by the perspectives of Buddhist and non-Buddhist philosophical views,

and which is uncorrupted by concepts,
the play of the three kāyas, thusness itself.

3.4 The Immediately Preceding Condition

At the time of engaging in the actual practice,
simply sustain the essence of the ordinary mind,
which is without thought of the object of meditation or the meditator,
and which is free from the fabrications of rejecting and adopting, and hope and doubt.

Part II: The Actual Practice

The actual practice has two parts: (1) śamatha and (2) vipaśyanā.

4. Śamatha

The presentation of śamatha is divided into the (1) general presentation and (2) detailed presentation.

4.1 A General Presentation of Śamatha

The general presentation of śamatha is divided into (1) the crucial points of the body and (2) the crucial points of the mind.

4.1.1 Crucial Points of the Body

The crucial points of the body refer
to the seven-point posture of Vairocana,
according to which one should sit on a comfortable cushion as follows:
1. feet in vajra posture,
2. hands placed evenly,
3. shoulders spread like vultures' wings,
4. neck drawn in like an iron hook,

5. spine straight like an arrow,
6. eyes focused on the space four finger-widths in front of the tip of the nose,
7. lips and teeth resting naturally, and tongue touching the upper palate.

4.1.2 Crucial Points of the Mind

The crucial points of the mind are,
as stated according to [Tilopa's six words of advice],
"Don't recall, don't imagine, don't think,
don't meditate, don't examine, rest naturally."
Rest in uncontrived ease, without grasping to luminosity or emptiness,
single-pointedly, loosely relaxed yet without distraction,
on the essence of this momentary ordinary mind,
which is free from refuting and affirming,
rejecting and adopting, hoping and doubting,
and free of adhering to true existence which reifies objects.

4.2 A Detailed Presentation of Śamatha

The detailed presentation of śamatha has three sections: (1) settling the mind that has not been settled, (2) stabilizing the mind that has been settled, and (3) enhancing the mind that has been stabilized.

4.2.1 Settling the Mind That Has Not Been Settled

Settling the mind that has not been settled has three subsections: (1) Concentrating with an object, (2) concentrating without an object, and (3) concentrating on the breath.

4.2.1.1 Concentrating with an Object

Concentrating with an object has two subsections: (1) focusing on external objects and (2) focusing on internal objects.

4.2.1.1.1 Focusing on External Objects

Focusing on external objects has two divisions: (1) concentrating on ordinary objects and (3) concentrating on extraordinary objects.

4.2.1.1.1.1 Concentrating on Ordinary Objects

Sit observing the proper gaze and the crucial points of the body.
Rest in single-pointed meditative equipoise,
and without wandering to any other object,
fix the mind on some coarse object in front of you, like a pillar or the wall.

Similarly, concentrate without wandering on some small object
in front of you, like a stick or a pebble.
Moreover, you can concentrate by taking as your focal object
a candle flame, space, or similarly
a pea-sized white drop at the point between the brows.

4.2.1.1.1.2 Concentrating on Extraordinary Objects

Visualize in front of you the perfect Buddha, the Bhagavan,
together with the appropriate color, clothing, marks, and signs,
and hold the mind there
with reverence, single-pointedly.

4.2.1.1.2 Focusing on Internal Objects

Generate whichever yidam is appropriate, or meditate on your guru
seated on an eight-petaled lotus at your heart,
or else visualize a luminous ball of light
that is in essence your yidam or guru and hold the mind on it.

Without wandering from these focal objects,
maintain the proper gaze and be free of the faults too tight and too loose.
Apart from the spy of mindfulness, remain in a state that is free of construction.
Without rejecting or adopting, hoping or doubting,
rest the mind just as it is, loosely relaxed, lightly, and unrestrained.

4.2.1.2 Concentrating without an Object

Concentrate instantaneously on the great emptiness
of all phenomena, both outer and inner objects,
or else dissolve those objects one into the other,
and set the mind in meditative equipoise on the great emptiness and luminosity.

4.2.1.3 Concentrating on the Breath

To concentrate on the breath, focus on vase-breathing,
or count the rounds of breath up to twenty-one, and so on,
counting each exhalation, inhalation, and retention as a single breath.
Strive for a long time with many repetitions without wandering,
maintaining clarity, lucidity, and intensity.

In that way, by meditating according to these oral instructions,
the following three stages will successively arise:
the first is like a waterfall on a cliff face,
the second is like a gently flowing river,
and the third is like an unfluctuating ocean.

4.2.2 Stabilizing the Mind That Has Been Settled

There are two subsections for stabilizing the mind that has been recognized: (1) holding the mind and (2) the ninefold method for resting the mind.

4.2.2.1 Holding the Mind

Holding the mind is threefold: (1) holding the mind above, (2) holding the mind below, and (3) the practice of alternating (holding the mind above and below).

4.2.2.1.1 Holding the Mind Above

Focus the mind and hold the wind within a pea-sized white drop
in the center of a four-petaled lotus at the heart.
As you expel the wind, the drop goes out through the aperture of Brahmā
and imagine that it remains in the expanse of space.

Strive at maintaining the proper gaze
and the crucial points of the body.
Uplift the mind and intensify your awareness;
in that way, meditate for a long time.

4.2.2.1.2 Holding the Mind Below

The second holding: in the center of a downward-facing
four-petaled black lotus is a pea-sized black drop.
Like the thread drawn from a spider, it spirals down
and is drawn out from the secret place.
It gradually descends, remaining heavily many fathoms beneath you.
Hold the mind single-pointedly on that, contract the anus,
and meditate maintaining the crucial points of the body and a downward gaze.

4.2.2.1.3 Holding the Mind Both Above and Below

Moreover, according to your assessment,
if your mind is too elevated, then hold below,
and if your mind is too low, then hold above.

Alternate the practice using these two focal objects [as appropriate], continually making effort, like the flow of a river.

4.2.2.2 Ninefold Method for Resting the Mind

(1) Placement, (2) continuous placement, (3) definite placement,
(4) close placement, (5) disciplining, (6) pacifying,
(7) thoroughly pacifying, (8) creating a single continuum, and (9) even placement.

The meaning of these is taught in succession:

1. [Placement:] Place the mind, fixing it single-pointedly on the focal object.
2. [Continuous placement:] Settle the mind on that object for a long time.
3. [Definite placement:] If thoughts arise, recognize that with your mindfulness immediately, and place the mind evenly.
4. [Close placement:] Place the mind evenly by mixing the mind of meditative equipoise with the previously settled mind.
5. [Disciplining:] Recalling the virtues of the settled mind, develop joy, and remain in that state.
6. [Pacifying:] Ascertain which conditions give rise to wandering, overcome attachment to those, and remain so.
7. [Thoroughly pacifying:] Recognize the nature of the causes of distraction and unhappiness, etc., and simply self-liberate them.
8. [Creating a single continuum:] Having meditated in that way, remain engaged with the focal object spontaneously and without depending on effort.
9. [Even placement:] Finally, be free of all distractions about whether or not one is in equipoise.

4.2.3 Enhancing the Mind That Has Been Stabilized

Focus your awareness on the forms of visual appearances,
and likewise, taking sound, etc., in succession
as your focal support, place the mind single-pointedly.
Moreover, whatever conceptual thoughts arise,
place the mind on them directly without viewing them as faults.
Alternately apply tightening and loosening,
and in particular, dispel obstacles and make progress.
Pray to the guru, and through your devotion,
the guru's mind and your own mind will become mixed as one.

5 Vipaśyanā

The section on vipaśyanā has three subsections: (1) looking at the nature of reality, the essence of mind, (2) cutting the fundamental root, and (3) introduction by determining awareness to be empty.

5.1 Looking at the Nature of Reality, the Essence of Mind

The way to look at the nature of reality, the essence of mind,
is to place the mind loosely relaxed just as it is, and without fabrication.
Examine and analyze [its] essence, color, shape, and so forth,
looking again and again.

The essence of the resting [mind]
should be luminous and naked, vivid alertness.
If, having searched for the resting [mind], you do not find it,
let it be free and analyze how it fluctuates.

5.2 Cutting the Fundamental Root

Then, as for showing how to cut the fundamental root:
when you search but do not find [the mind],
search again and again by properly analyzing
the searcher and how the mind arises, abides, and departs, etc.

Moreover, the eleven mental applications are
(1) thorough searching, (2) individual examination, (3) detailed analysis,
(4) śamatha, (5) vipaśyanā, (6) union [of śamatha and vipaśyanā],
(7) clarity, (8) nonconceptuality, (9) equanimity,
(10) uninterrupted continuity, (11) nondistraction.

The meaning of these is taught respectively as follows:

1. [Thorough searching:] Search continuously for the mental continuum, [inquiring,] "Does the mind exist or not, and what is its essence like?"
2. [Individual examination:] In particular, cut the fundamental root, [examining] the color, shape, etc., the arising, abiding, departing, and the foundation.
3. [Detailed analysis:] Search for the ultimate status of that which is sought and the searcher.
4. [Śamatha:] Having realized that the mind has no nature by having searched for it,
   in order to determine the nature of reality of all phenomena as well,
   rest the mind on the profound meaning.
5. [Vipaśyanā:] By searching for the essence of that previous resting itself, thoroughly realize the very nature.
6. [Union of śamatha and vipaśyanā:] Those two are nondistinct and indistinguishable.
7. [Clarity:] If you become dull and drowsy,
   then stimulate and uplift the mind.
8. [Nonconceptuality:] If you become scattered and agitated,
   then strive at the methods of pacification.
9. [Equanimity:] Once you have become free of dullness and agitation,
   rest in the essence of [the mind that was] sought, examined, and analyzed.

10. [Uninterrupted continuity:] Never be separated from such a practice.
11. [Nondistraction:] Having concentrated the mind on this, wandering will never find an opportunity.

By means of these eleven mental applications, exert yourself again and again at the method for cutting the fundamental root.

5.3 Introduction by Determining Awareness to Be Empty

As for the method of introduction by determining awareness to be empty:
Firstly, relax and rest the mind in its natural state.
Look nakedly at the essence of the relaxed mind.
Rely continuously on mindfulness that is completely undistracted.

No matter what conceptual thoughts arise,
do not engage in any kind of fabrication, including rejecting and adopting.
Rest with lucid alertness on the momentary ordinary mind,
the ungraspable, vivid wakefulness of luminous emptiness.

As for how to give introduction, there are two divisions: (1) introduction on the basis of movement and (2) introduction on the basis of appearance.

5.3.1 Introduction on the Basis of Movement

Moreover, as for the method of introduction on the basis of movement,
initially, rest awareness loosely in its natural state.
From within that state, look at its essence.
Then, bring about [mental] movement, and once more [inquire],
"What is the difference between the moving mind and the resting mind?"

Through looking for the difference between
the moving mind and the mind that is looking at it,
the movement is self-liberated.
Rest single-pointedly in that state without wandering.

5.3.2 Introducing on the Basis of Appearance

Introduction on the basis of appearance has four subsections: (1) introducing appearance as the mind, (2) introducing the mind itself as empty, (3) introducing emptiness as spontaneity, and (4) introducing spontaneity as self-liberated.

5.3.2.1 Introducing Appearance as the Mind

By examining whether mind and its
focal objects, such as forms, are the same or different,
once you realize that all objects appearing as external are not established
as anything other than the natural radiance of the mind,
rest openly in that state without grasping.

5.3.2.2 Introducing Mind Itself as Empty

Mind itself is not established at all, but is emptiness.
It cannot be conveyed by any means.
It is beyond words, thoughts, and expression, like space.
Rest naturally in that state without fabricating.

5.3.2.3 Introducing Emptiness as Spontaneous

Unmoving from the empty dharmatā,
the unceasing expressivity and radiance in fact dawns as the variety [of appearances].

All the phenomenal appearances of saṃsāra and nirvāṇa are nothing other than emptiness.
Spontaneity should be known as the inseparability of appearance and emptiness.

5.3.2.4 Introducing Spontaneity as Self-Liberated

Likewise, the three of appearance, awareness, and emptiness
have primordially been the spontaneity of the union of luminosity and emptiness.
Without relying on the antidotes of adopting or discarding, eliminating or adding,
that ultimate self-liberation is mahāmudrā.

Part III: Conclusion

6. How to Develop One's Capacity and Make Progress
6.1 Making Progress by Dispelling the Five Misconceptions
6.1.1 How to Eliminate Misconceptions with Respect to the Object

Through taking all phenomena included within dualism—
such as the object to be abandoned, saṃsāra,
and the object to be accomplished, nirvāṇa,
fixation and nongrasping, virtue and vice, etc.—
to be of an equal taste in the sphere of nondual wisdom,
one eliminates misconceptions with respect to objects.

6.1.2 How to Eliminate Misconceptions with Respect to Time

While the three times are not truly established,
the division of the three times is imputed by delusion.

Thus, given that the three times are not established as distinct,
through realizing their equality,
one eliminates misconceptions with respect to time.

6.1.3 How to Eliminate Misconceptions with Respect to the Essence

It is incorrect to assert that wisdom is obtained
subsequent to renouncing the present mind.
Through understanding that one's mind has been primordially
in the nature of the five wisdoms,
one eliminates misconceptions with respect to the essence.

6.1.4 How to Eliminate Misconceptions with Respect to the Nature

All the aggregates, constituents, and sense spheres of all sentient beings exist
in the nature of the tathāgatas, male and female, gods and goddesses.
Through understanding this,
one eliminates misconceptions with respect to the nature.

6.1.5 How to Eliminate Misconceptions with Respect to Knowledge

The ultimate is not an object of
high knowledge or rationality.
It is realized by means of the blessing of the guru
and fortune ones with good karmic momentum.
That realization eliminates misconceptions with respect to knowledge.

6.2 Training in the Three Skills

6.2.1 At the Beginning: Skill at Commencing Meditation

Properly maintaining the crucial points of the body, look for the essence;
when active, look on the basis of the activity,
and when still, look on the basis of the stillness.
Rest on just that awareness of one's own nature without wandering
from the unfabricated fresh natural state just as it is.

6.2.2 In the Middle: Skill at Ceasing Meditation

Whatever your object of meditative equipoise,
do not concern yourself primarily with the duration.
Adjusting your meditative concentration and the crucial points of the body,
meditate in many short sessions, maintaining lucidity and intensity,
and you will not become resentful [of your practice] but will remain inspired.

6.2.3 In the End: Skill at Sustaining the Experience

Whichever of the three meditative experiences dawn—bliss, clarity, or nonconceptuality—
since it is said that if you develop attachment to or pride about them
you will lose realization for the sake of meditative experience,
you should sustain [your meditation] in a state devoid of attachment to meditative experience.

6.3 Making Progress through Eliminating Deviations and Pitfalls
6.3.1 Eliminating Deviations
6.3.1.1 Deviation from Emptiness as the Nature of the Object of Knowledge

Having determined the fundamental nature of things to be empty
by means of the conventions involved in

listening to and contemplating scripture and reasoning, one may think,
"Since all things are empty, what reason is there to meditate?"
Since this is posited by intellectual construction, it is incorrect.

6.3.1.2 Deviation from Emptiness as the Seal

The "deviation from emptiness as the seal"
refers to holding that all things are not empty,
but that they become empty by articulating the śūnyatā mantra, etc.
It is also not correct to meditate in this way.

6.3.1.3 Deviation from Emptiness as the Antidote

The "deviation from emptiness as the antidote"
refers to engaging in meditative equipoise thinking,
"When thoughts such as the three poisons arise,
I will destroy them with emptiness." This is flawed.

6.3.1.4 Deviation from Emptiness as the Path

The "deviation from emptiness as the path"
refers to thinking, "While the path and the result are nondual in terms of emptiness,
I practice the path now by meditating on emptiness,
and later I will obtain the result." This is incorrect.

6.3.2 Making Progress by Avoiding Pitfalls to Meditation

As for the method for making progress by avoiding pitfalls,
seventeen points will be explained in sequence:

1. From among the three of bliss, luminosity, and nonconceptuality, as for the meditative experience of bliss,

intellectually examining bliss in general
without distinguishing between contaminated and uncontaminated bliss [is the first pitfall].

2. If you become completely attached [to that bliss] while meditating on it,
you will stray into the desire realm.
3. Likewise, if you are attached to the meditative experience
of luminosity, you will stray into the form realm.
4. If you are attached to nonconceptuality,
you will be born in the formless realm.

5. Moreover, if you become completely attached to the discerning analysis
that "all phenomena are like space,"
you will be born in the sphere of limitless space.
6. Due to holding to the thought that "phenomena are [in fact] the mind,"
you will stray into the sphere of limitless consciousness.
7. If you become attached to the thought that nothing is established,
then you will stray in the sphere of nothingness.
8. If you become attached to the thought that there is neither existence nor nonexistence,
then you will be reborn in the sphere of neither discernment nor nondiscernment.

9. Thus, be free from desire and attachment
for the meditative experiences of bliss, luminosity, and nonconceptuality,
all [these pitfalls] will be avoided
by seeing the true face of the natural state.

10. Since it is by attachment to emptiness while lacking method,
that one strays into the lower way,

the method for eliminating this [pitfall] is to meditate
on love, compassion, and bodhicitta.

11. With method, you will make progress in knowledge.
12. With knowledge, you will make progress in method.
13. With the union of those two,
progress in one helps you make progress in the other.

14. Developing vipaśyanā progresses śamatha.
15. Developing śamatha also progresses vipaśyanā.

16. With respect to both śamatha and vipaśyanā,
at the level of single-pointedness, developing meditative experience
progresses meditative experience.
Similarly, at the level of freedom from proliferation,
developing meditative experience progresses realization.
At the level of one taste, developing realization
progresses realization.
By transforming all ordinary actions of the three doors
without exception into a variety of virtues,
you will make progress at [transforming] the ordinary into excellent qualities.

17. Looking at the true face of faults, such as mental afflictions, suffering, and obstacles,
without discarding or adopting,
by taking bad omens to be auspicious, you will make progress.

6.4 Making Progress by Crossing the Three Dangerous Passes

6.4.1 Emptiness Arising as One's Enemy

When you analyze and look at the essence of mind,
having seen that nothing whatsoever is established,

you may fail to apprehend that which is to be rejected and its antidote,
thinking, "Since all phenomena are merely emptiness,
virtue and vice, cause and effect, and so on, are also not established."
This is known as "deluded chatter";
it is emptiness arising as one's enemy
and should be rejected like poison.

6.4.2 Compassion Arising as One's Enemy

Once you have acquired a little bliss of meditative concentration,
you may think, "I will liberate sentient beings who do not have that."
Then, having given up the practice of meditative concentration,
you may exert yourself at various acts of virtue
and conceive of them to be truly existent;
this is known as "compassion arising as one's enemy."
In a state inseparable from the arising of compassion,
strive to sustain your stainless realization.

6.4.3 Cause and Result Arising as One's Enemy

If, thinking, "In order to realize the profound nature of reality,
I must become learned in all fields of knowledge,"
you undertake the study of grammar, epistemology, and so forth,
and give up the practice of śamatha and vipaśyanā,
this is known as "the thought of cause and effect arising as one's enemy";
it is incorrect.
Thus, by meditating single-pointedly on the profound meaning,
you will obtain the undeluded stainless knowledge of
all phenomenal appearances in saṃsāra and nirvāṇa.

7. How to Eliminate Obstacles

7.1 Eliminating Obstacles of Sickness

Through primarily practicing śamatha, wind diseases are
eliminated.
Through practicing vipaśyanā, diseases of phlegm and bile are
eliminated.
Moreover, diseases related to heat and cold are gradually eliminated
by practicing both śamatha and vipaśyanā.

Likewise, examine the essence of whatever sickness you have:
its shape, its source, and where it goes.
In particular, make special effort at sending and taking (*tonglen*).

Alternatively: The nonarising of illness is the dharmakāya.
Its nonabiding is the saṃbhogakāya. Its nonceasing is the
nirmāṇakāya.
Its empty nature is the svabhāvakāya.
Taking [illness] to be the play of the four kāyas, look at its true face.

7.2 Eliminating Demonic Obstacles

Likewise, as for the way to eliminate demonic obstacles:
The appearance of demons is the magical play of the mind.
Take the mind itself to be the four kāyas
and eliminate demons too by means of
taking them into the path of the four kāyas.

7.3 Eliminating Obstacles to Meditative Concentration

In general, the method for eliminating the faults
of dullness and agitation is as previously explained.
Now, to eliminate [these] by means of guru yoga:

When you [experience] dullness, [visualize] Guru Amitābha on your crown;
the lineage gurus and so forth dissolve into him,
and by virtue of invoking him with devotion,
light rays emanate and dissolve into you,
whereupon the causes for dullness are completely purified.
The guru melts into light and dissolves into you,
whereby your body transforms into a ball of light,
and the entire pure realm is made manifest,
whereupon it dissolves into space.
Rest the mind lucidly, with intensified awareness.

If you [experience] agitation, visualize guru Vajrasattva, blue in color,
In the middle of a four-petaled lotus at your heart;
on the four petals are Vairocana, and so forth, the same in color,
surrounded by the *vīras*, ḍākinīs, and so forth belonging to their families.
Visualize blue light emanating from their hearts
piercing the guru, and light rays spread in all directions.
Eliminate [agitation] by resting in equipoise in the state of mahāmudrā.

Moreover, whichever of dullness or agitation occurs, rest naturally
on its essence without wandering, without meditating, without contrivance.

8. How to Traverse the Path

8.1 Teaching How to Traverse Higher and Higher on the Path by Way of the Four Yogas

8.1.1 The First Yoga: Single-Pointedness

Firstly, as for the yoga of single-pointedness:
awareness of the true nature of mind,

remains clearly and lucidly in the state
of space-like unceasing luminosity and emptiness, without center or limit.

Dividing that into lesser, middling, and superior:
The lesser is seeing the essence of bliss and luminosity.
The middling is attaining mastery in meditative concentration.
The superior is meditative experience becoming constant.

8.1.2 The Second Yoga: Freedom from Fabrication

Freedom from fabrication is the realization that the mind itself is ungrounded.
Having become liberated from fabrications
concerning the arising, ceasing, and abiding
of all dualistic phenomena,
and from grasping at characteristics,
cut superimpositions concerning unborn emptiness.

The lesser [level] is the realization that one's mind is unarisen.
The middling is freedom from the fundamental root
of grasping at appearances and grasping at emptiness.
The superior is cutting the superimpositions that fabricate all phenomena.

8.1.4 The Third Yoga: One Taste

The yoga of one taste is the mixing of appearances and mind.
All phenomenal appearances of saṃsāra and nirvāṇa,
are equal in terms of the natural state,
neither free nor unfree from the fabrication of arising and ceasing,
neither empty nor nonempty,
neither negated nor established, neither discarded nor adopted.

The lesser [level] is the mixing into one equal taste
of all phenomena included in both [saṃsāra and nirvāṇa].
The middling is when appearance and mind are like water poured into water.
The superior is when all phenomena are pacified in the state of equality.

8.1.5 The Fourth Yoga: Nonmeditation

Nonmeditation is the purification of one's earlier meditative experiences
or the utter cessation of the intellectual mind.
That has lesser, middling, and superior levels:
The lesser is when there is no object of meditation or meditator.
The middling is when you have taken hold of the natural place of spontaneity.
The superior is when, having mixed the mother and son clear light,
and having become diffused into the expanse of wisdom, the dharmadhātu,
one accomplishes the two aims and attains complete enlightenment.

8.2 The Twelve Stages: Dividing Each of the Four Yogas into the Three of Lesser, Middling, and Superior

If one were to correspond the twelve yogas
to the grounds and paths according to the perfection of wisdom:

Lesser single-pointedness is the path of accumulation.
Middling is the heat and peak levels of the path of preparation.
Superior single-pointedness is the forbearance and supreme attribute levels of the path of preparation.

Lesser freedom from fabrication is the path of seeing, the first bodhisattva level.

Middling is from the second to the fifth bodhisattva levels.
At the time of the superior, the sixth bodhisattva level is attained.

Through the realization of lesser one taste, one [reaches] the seventh bodhisattva level.
Middling is the eighth bodhisattva level.
Superior one taste corresponds to the ninth bodhisattva level.

Lesser nonmeditation corresponds to the tenth bodhisattva level.
Middling is the limit of the continuum.
Superior is the completion of the path, corresponding to the eleventh bodhisattva level.

9. How to Actualize the Result

In that way, once the twelve yogas have progressively arisen
in one's mental continuum and nonmeditation is accomplished,
the two obscurations and the entirety of karmic imprints will be eradicated
and the fruition of the wisdom of the two knowledges will be completed.
Though not moving from the dharmakāya for one's own sake,
for the sake of others, the rūpakāya will enact the benefit of beings
until saṃsāra is empty,
without conceptual thought, effort, striving, or proliferations,
with continuous enlightened activity
and the spontaneous presence of the pervasive nature.

9.1 Dedication

By virtue of this effort and the merit acquired here,
in this life and in all lives to come,
may I properly remain in a state of renunciation of saṃsāra,

and may I never transgress even the slightest of the fundamental
precepts!

May I never forget even in my dreams the two bodhicittas that benefit others,
and using the four means for gathering disciples
and the practice of the six perfections,
may I establish all beings in bliss!

May I cherish qualified spiritual guides
as I do my own life,
and pleasing them with all kinds of service,
may I always have faith and maintain my samaya.

In dependence on the power of this [virtue], with respect to the entire tripiṭaka—
the pratimokṣa, bodhisattva, and Mantrayāna of the knowledge holders—
for my own sake, may I listen, contemplate, and meditate.
For the sake of others, may I teach, debate, and compose treatises.
For both myself and others, may I become learned, disciplined, and good hearted.
For the sake of the teachings, may I uphold, protect, and propagate them.
May all this be fully accomplished!

Having gained realization in accordance
with the treatises on the irreversible definitive meaning,
and particularly the natural state of mahāmudrā,
may I become the one to spread it!

In summary, may I alone be able to establish
all beings without exception

filling the extent of space
in the state of complete and perfect buddhahood!

With the blessings of the triple gem
and the power of my pure superior intention,
and through the force of the profound emptiness and dependent origination,
may all these aspirations be achieved just so!

Since the *Essential Root Verses on the Points of Meditation* that I compiled from the *Instruction Manual on the Quintessential Nectar of the Six Yogas* by the Sixth Shamar Chökyi Wangchuk is helpful for practicing meditation and recitation, I have been intending to do something similar for Mahāmudrā. Now, while both Nedo Kuchung Choktrul Rinpoche and Dilyak Lama Tsethar have been in three-year retreat, they have been printing the above-mentioned root verses on the six yogas, and saying that they wish for something similar for the practice of Mahāmudrā, they ardently requested this of me. I have composed this with the superior intention of wishing to benefit, in some small respect, beginning practitioners.

This was written by Bokar Tulku Karma Ngedön Chökyi Lodrö, the retreat master of Yi'ong Samten Ling at the great monastic seat of Gyalwai Wangpo Pal Karmapa, Ogmin Shedrup Chökhor Ling. It was composed at Bokar Ngedön Chökhor Ling in the peaceful place of medicinal herbs, Mirik, Darjeeling, on December 13, 1984, the twentieth day of the tenth month of the wood mouse year, on the date of the auspicious conjunction of Jupiter and Puṣya and the elements of fire and wind. May virtuous goodness increase!

12. TIBETAN TEXT

༄། །ཕྱག་ཆེན་ངེས་དོན་རྒྱ་མཚོའི་བསྡུས་དོན་རྩ་ཚིག་ཁྲིར་བདེར་བཀོད་པ་ངེས་དོན་སྒོ་འབྱེད་ཅེས་བྱ་བ་བཞུགས་སོ། །

༄། །ཨོཾ་སྭ་སྟི། །བླ་མ་ལྷ་དང་རང་སེམས་རྣམས། །
དབྱེར་མེད་གཉུག་མའི་ངང་དུ་གཅིག །
དེ་ལ་བདག་ནི་དུས་ཀུན་དུ། །
ཕྱག་འཚལ་སྐྱབས་སུ་ཉེ་བར་མཆི། །

དེ་ལ་འདིར་གང་དག་ཕྱག་རྒྱ་ཆེན་པོ་ལྷན་ཅིག་སྐྱེས་སྦྱོར་གྱི་ཁྲིད་ངེས་དོན་རྒྱ་མཚོ་ལ་འཇུག་པ་འདོད་པ་དེ་དག་ལ་ཕན་པའི་བློས་གཞུང་གི་ས་བཅད་རྣམས་ཟུར་དུ་བཀོལ་ཅིང་། དེ་དང་དེའི་ཐད་ཀྱི་སྒོམ་རིམ་རྣམས་གཟུང་བདེ་བའི་ཕྱིར། བསྡུས་དོན་རྩ་ཚིག་ལྟ་བུའམ་འདོན་སྒོམ་སྦྲག་མར་བྱས་ཀྱང་རུང་བའི་ཉུང་གསལ་ཞིག་སྤེལ་བར་བྱའོ། དེ་ལ་སྔོན་འགྲོ་དང་། དངོས་གཞི། རྗེས་གསུམ་ལས། དང་པོ་སྔོན་འགྲོ་ལ། ཐུན་མོང་གི་སྔོན་འགྲོ་དང་། ཐུན་མོང་མ་ཡིན་པའི་སྔོན་འགྲོ་ཁྱད་པར་གྱི་སྔོན་འགྲོ་དང་གསུམ་ལས། དང་པོ་ཐུན་མོང་གི་སྔོན་འགྲོ་ལ་བཞི་སྟེ། དལ་འབྱོར་རྙེད་དཀའ། འཆི་བ་མི་རྟག་པ། ལས་རྒྱུ་འབྲས། འཁོར་བའི་ཉེས་དམིགས་སྒོམ་པའོ།

དང་པོ་ནི།
ན་མོ་གུ་རུ་བྷྱཿགང་ཞིག་དམ་ཆོས་ཚུལ་བཞིན་སྒྲུབ་པ་ལ། །
རྣམ་གཡེང་སྤང་སྟེ་ཐོག་མར་བསྒོམ་བྱ་ནི། །
དལ་བརྒྱད་འབྱོར་པ་བཅུ་ལྡན་རྟེན་བཟང་འདི། །
རྙེད་པར་དཀའ་ཞིང་ཕན་ཐོགས་ཆེས་ཆེ་བས། །

ཡིད་བཞིན་ནུར་བུ་དང་ནི་ཆོས་མཚུངས་ཤིང་།།
ཁྱད་པར་རྡོ་རྗེ་ཐེག་པ་ལ་བརྟེན་ནས།།
ཚེ་གཅིག་བྱང་ཆུབ་སྒྲུབ་ལ་ཁམས་དྲུག་ལྡན།།
རྡོ་རྗེའི་ལུས་འདི་དེ་བས་ཀྱང་ནི་དཀོན།།
དེ་ཡང་རྒྱུ་དང་དཔེ་དང་གྲངས་གསུམ་གྱིས།།
རྙེད་པར་དཀའ་ཞིང་རྙེད་ཀྱང་ཆེས་ཤིན་ཏུ།།
འཇིག་པར་སླ་བས་ད་རེས་ནས་བཟུང་སྟེ།།
དམ་ཆོས་གཤའ་མ་སྒྲུབ་ལ་འབད་པར་བྱ།།

གཉིས་པ་ནི།

ཕྱི་ནང་སྣོད་བཅུད་འདུས་བྱས་ཆོས་ཐམས་ཅད།།
མཐའ་བཞིའི་ཚུལ་གྱིས་སྐད་ཅིག་ཀྱང་མི་རྟག།
ཁྱད་པར་འགྲོ་བའི་ཚེ་སྲོག་རླུང་གསེབ་ཀྱི།།
མར་མེ་དང་ནི་ཆུ་ཡི་ཆུ་བུར་བཞིན།།

དེ་ཡང་བདག་ཉིད་ངེས་པར་འཆི་བ་དང་།།
ནམ་འཆི་ཆ་མེད་པར་ནི་མྱུར་དུ་འཆི།།
འཆི་རྐྱེན་མང་ཞིང་མི་འདོད་བཞིན་དུ་འཆི།།
དེ་ལ་གང་གིས་ཀྱང་ནི་ཟློག་མི་ནུས།།

འཆི་ཚེ་སྡུག་བསྔལ་བཟོད་གླག་མེད་སྨྲོང་ཞིང་།།
དེ་ཚེ་དམ་པའི་ཆོས་ལས་སྐྱབས་གཞན་མེད།།
དེས་ན་བློ་སྣ་བསྐྱུངས་ཤིང་སྐྱོ་ཤས་བསྐྱེད།།
ལོང་མེད་བསམ་པ་དྲག་པོས་དགེ་ལ་འབུངས།།

གསུམ་པ་ནི།

འཆི་རྗེས་སྣུམ་ཟད་མར་མེ་ལྟ་བུའམ།།
ཡང་ན་གར་སྐྱེ་རང་དབང་ཡོད་མིན་ཏེ།།
དབང་མེད་ལས་ཀྱི་རྗེས་སུ་ངེས་པར་འབྲངས།།
ཕྱིར་ན་བདེ་སྡུག་སྣང་བ་སྣ་ཚོགས་པ།།

དགེ་སྡིག་ལས་ཀྱི་འབྲས་བུ་ཡིན་པར་གསུངས། །
དེ་ཡང་དགེ་བཅུ་སྤྱད་ལས་བདེ་འགྲོ་དང་། །
ཉོན་མོངས་དབང་གིས་མི་དགེ་བཅུ་སྤྱད་པས། །
ངན་འགྲོར་སྐྱེ་བའི་ཚུལ་སོགས་ཞིབ་ཏུ་བསམ། །

མདོར་ན་རང་གིས་བྱས་པའི་རྣམ་སྨིན་ནི། །
ཚད་དུ་མི་ཟ་ནམ་ཞིག་རང་ཉིད་ཀྱིས། །
སྤྱོད་བར་ངེས་པས་དགེ་སྡིག་བླང་དོར་ཀུན། །
ཚུལ་བཞིན་འབད་ལ་རང་རྒྱུད་གཞིག་འགྲོལ་བྱོས། །

བཞི་པ་ནི།
ཁམས་གསུམ་འཁོར་བ་རིགས་དྲུག་གར་སྐྱེས་ཀྱང་། །
སྡུག་བསྔལ་གསུམ་གྱིས་རྟག་ཏུ་རབ་མནར་ཏེ། །
དེ་ཡང་ཤིན་ཏུ་དོས་དྲག་ཡུན་རིང་བོར། །
དམྱལ་བ་ཚ་གྲང་ཡི་དྭགས་བཀྲེས་སྐོམ་དང་། །

དུད་འགྲོ་གཅིག་ལ་གཅིག་ཟའི་སྡུག་བསྔལ་དང་། །
མི་ལ་སྐྱེ་རྒ་ན་འཆི་སོགས་དེ་བཞིན། །
ལྷ་མིན་འཐབ་རྩོད་ལྷ་ལ་འཕོ་ལྟུང་གི །
སྡུག་བསྔལ་དེ་རྣམས་སྤྱོད་བའི་ཚུལ་བསམ་སྟེ། །

ལྟར་སྣང་སྲིད་པའི་བདེ་འབྱོར་ཕྲ་མོ་འདི། །
དུག་དང་སྦྱར་བའི་ཟས་བཞིན་རིང་དུ་དོར། །
འཁོར་བ་མེ་འོབས་དང་འདྲ་འདི་ལས་ནི། །
ངེས་པར་ཐར་བའི་ཐབས་ཤིག་ད་རེས་རེམ། །

གཉིས་པ་ཐུན་མོང་མ་ཡིན་པའི་སྔོན་འགྲོ་བཞི་སྦྱོར་ནི། རྒྱུད་སྡོད་དུ་ཐུང་བའམ་ཅི་བྱས་ཐར་པའི་ལམ་དུ་འགྲོ་བ་སྐྱབས་འགྲོ་སེམས་བསྐྱེད་ཀྱི་ཁྲིད་དང་། སྡིག་སྒྲིབ་དག་པར་བྱེད་པ་རྡོ་རྗེ་སེམས་དཔའི་སྒོམ་བཟླས། ཚོགས་གཉིས་རྫོགས་པར་བྱེད་པ་མཎྜལ། བྱིན་རླབས་མྱུར་དུ་འཇུག་པར་བྱེད་པ་བླ་མའི་རྣལ་འབྱོར་གྱི་ཁྲིད་དོ།

དང་པོ་ནི།

དེ་ལྟར་སྲིད་པའི་སྡུག་བསྔལ་ལས་སྐྱོབ་པའི། །
སྐྱབས་ནི་དཀོན་མཆོག་གསུམ་ལས་གཞན་མ་མཆིས། །
དེས་ན་བདག་གཞན་མཁའ་ཁྱབ་འགྲོ་བ་ཀུན། །
སྐྱབས་སུ་འགྲོ་ལ་འདི་ལྟར་གསལ་གདབ་སྟེ། །

མདུན་མཁར་དཔག་བསམ་ལྗོན་ཤིང་ཡལ་ག་ལྔ། །
གྱེས་པའི་དབུས་མར་སེང་ཁྲི་པད་ཟླའི་སྟེང་། །
རྩ་བའི་བླ་མ་རྡོ་རྗེ་འཆང་དབང་ནི། །
མཚན་དཔེས་རབ་རྫོགས་ལྷམ་མེ་ལྷན་ནེར་བཞུགས། །

དེ་སྟེང་བརྒྱུད་པའི་བླ་མ་ཐོ་བརྩེགས་དང་། །
མདུན་གཡས་རྒྱབ་དང་གཡོན་དུ་རིམ་པ་བཞིན། །
ཡི་དམ་སངས་རྒྱས་ཆོས་དང་དགེ་འདུན་རྣམས། །
སྤྲིན་གྱི་ཕུང་པོ་གཏིབས་བཞིན་བཞུགས་པ་ལ། །

བདག་སོགས་འགྲོ་ཀུན་རྫོགས་བྱང་མ་ཐོབ་བར། །
སྐྱབས་སུ་འགྲོ་ཞིང་བྱང་ཆུབ་སེམས་མཆོག་བསྐྱེད། །
མཐའ་མར་སྐྱབས་ཡུལ་འོད་ཞུ་བདག་ཉིད་ཀྱི། །
སྒོ་གསུམ་ལ་ཐིམ་གཉུག་མའི་རང་ངོར་ཞོག །

གཉིས་པ་ནི།

ཐོག་མེད་ནས་བསགས་སྡིག་ལྟུང་ཅི་མཆིས་ཀུན། །
སྟོབས་བཞིའི་སྒོ་ནས་བཤགས་ཤིང་ཁྱད་པར་དུ། །
གཉེན་པོ་ཀུན་ཏུ་སྤྱོད་པའི་སྟོབས་ཀྱི་མཆོག །
རྡོ་རྗེ་སེམས་དཔའི་སྒོམ་བཟླས་ལ་འཇུག་ན། །

རང་ཉིད་ཐ་མལ་གནས་པའི་སྤྱི་གཙུག་ཏུ། །
བླ་མ་རྡོ་རྗེ་སེམས་དཔའ་སྐུ་མདོག་དཀར། །
ཕྱག་གཡས་རྡོ་རྗེ་རྩེ་ལྔ་ཐུགས་ཀར་འཛིན། །
གཡོན་པས་དྲིལ་བུ་དཀུར་རྟེན་སེམས་སྐྱིལ་བཞུགས། །

སྣང་ལ་རང་བཞིན་མེད་པའི་སྐུར་གསལ་བའི། །
ཐུགས་ཀར་ཟླ་སྟེང་ཧཱུྃ་ལ་ཡིག་བརྒྱས་བསྐོར། །
དེ་ལས་བདུད་རྩིའི་རྒྱུན་བབས་ཚང་བུག་ནས། །
ཞུགས་ཏེ་སྒྲིབ་པ་ཉམས་ཆག་མ་ལུས་སྦྱངས། །

སླར་ཡང་གསོལ་བ་བཏབ་པས་དགྱེས་བཞིན་དུ། །
ཁྱོད་ཀྱི་སྡིག་སྒྲིབ་ཐམས་ཅད་དག་གོ་ཞེས། །
གསུང་གི་དབུགས་དབྱུང་དང་བཅས་འོད་དུ་ཞུ། །
རང་ཐིམ་རྡོ་རྗེ་གསུམ་དང་དབྱེར་མེད་གྱུར། །

གསུམ་པ་ནི།
ཞིང་ཁམས་འབུལ་བའི་ཐབས་མཆོག་ལ་བརྟེན་ནས། །
བསོད་ནམས་ཡེ་ཤེས་ཚོགས་གཉིས་གསོག་པར་བྱ། །
དེ་ལ་སྐྱོན་གྱི་དྲི་མས་མ་གོས་པའི། །
རིན་ཆེན་ལས་གྲུབ་སྤུབ་པའི་མཎྜལ་ཉིད། །

མཚན་ཉིད་ཡོངས་རྫོགས་གཞལ་ཡས་ཁང་གསལ་བའི། །
དབུས་སུ་རྩ་བའི་བླ་མ་ཕྱོགས་བཞི་རུ། །
ཡི་དམ་སངས་རྒྱས་ཆོས་དང་དགེ་འདུན་དང་། །
དཔའ་བོ་མཁའ་འགྲོ་ཡེ་ཤེས་སྲུང་མར་བཅས། །

ལེགས་པར་གསལ་བཏབ་རང་ཉིད་དེའི་མདུན་དུ། །
མཆོད་པའི་མཎྜལ་ཐོགས་ཏེ་རི་རབ་དང་། །
གླིང་བཞི་གླིང་ཕྲན་ལ་སོགས་བྱེ་བ་བརྒྱ། །
གཞན་ཡང་བདག་སོགས་མཁའ་མཉམ་འགྲོ་ཀུན་གྱི། །

ལུས་དང་ལོངས་སྤྱོད་དགེ་ཚོགས་ཅི་མཆིས་ཀུན། །
མ་ལུས་བློ་ཡིས་བླངས་ཏེ་ཕུལ་བའི་མཐུས། །
ཚོགས་གཉིས་རབ་རྫོགས་ལྷ་རྣམས་དགྱེས་པའི་ངང་། །
འོད་ཞུ་རང་ལ་ཐིམ་པས་གཉིས་མེད་གྱུར། །

བཞི་པ་ནི།
ཡོན་ཏན་ཀུན་གྱི་གཞིར་གྱུར་ཁྱད་པར་དུ། །
དོན་དམ་ཕྱག་ཆེན་རྟོགས་པའི་ཐབས་མཆོག་ནི། །
དཔལ་ལྡན་བླ་མའི་བྱིན་རླབས་ལས་གཞན་མེད། །
དེ་ཕྱིར་དེ་ཡི་རྣལ་འབྱོར་བྱ་བ་ལ། །

རང་ཉིད་ཡི་དམ་ལྷར་གསལ་སྤྱི་གཙུག་ཏུ། །
རྩ་བའི་བླ་མ་རྡོ་རྗེ་འཆང་དབང་པོ། །
དེ་སྟེང་བརྒྱུད་པའི་བླ་མ་རྣམས་ཐོ་བརྩེགས། །
གཞན་ཡང་ཡི་དམ་སངས་རྒྱས་བྱང་ཆུབ་དང་། །

དཔའ་བོ་མཁའ་འགྲོ་ཡེ་ཤེས་སྲུང་མས་བསྐོར། །
དེ་ལ་མཆོད་ཅིང་གདུང་བས་གསོལ་བཏབ་མཐུས། །
འཁོར་རྣམས་གཙོར་ཐིམ་གཙོ་བོ་དེ་ཉིད་ནི། །
སྐྱབས་གནས་ཀུན་འདུས་ཉིད་གྱུར་སླར་ཡང་དེར། །

དབང་བསྐུར་གསོལ་བ་བཏབ་པས་དབང་བཞི་ཐོབ། །
སྒྲིབ་བཞི་དག་ཅིང་སྐུ་བཞིའི་ས་བོན་བཞག །
དེ་ནས་བླ་མ་དགྱེས་བཞིན་འོད་དུ་ཞུ། །
རང་ཐིམ་ཕྱག་ཆེན་ངང་དུ་མཉམ་པར་ཞོག །

གསུམ་པ་ཁྱད་པར་གྱི་སྔོན་འགྲོ་བཞི་ནི། རྒྱུའི་རྐྱེན་དང་། བདག་པོའི་རྐྱེན། དམིགས་པའི་རྐྱེན། དེ་མ་ཐག་པའི་རྐྱེན་དང་བཞི་ལས།

དང་པོ་ནི།
རང་རྒྱུད་ལེགས་པར་དུལ་ཅིང་ངེས་འབྱུང་དང་། །
ཐར་འདོད་བསམ་པས་ཞེན་ཁྲིས་ཀུན་བཅད་དེ། །
ཤིན་ཏུ་དབེན་པའི་གནས་སུ་ཕྱི་ནང་གི །
རྣམ་གཡེང་མེད་པར་བྱ་བཏང་པོ་ནར་གནས། །

གཉིས་པ་ནི། ཕྱག་རྒྱ་ཆེན་པོ་རྟོགས་པར་བྱེད་པའི་ལམ་བླ་མ་ཁོ་ན་ལ་རག་ལས་པས། ཡང་དག་པའི་དགེ་བའི་བཤེས་གཉེན་གྱིས་ཟིན་པ་ཞིག་དགོས་ཤིང་། དེ་ལའང་གང་ཟག་བརྒྱུད་པའི་བླ་མ། བདེ་གཤེགས་བཀའི་བླ་མ། སྣང་བ་བརྡའི་བླ་མ། དོན་དམ་ཆོས་ཉིད་ཀྱི་བླ་མ་དང་བཞི་ལས།

དང་པོ་ནི།

རྡོ་རྗེ་འཆང་ནས་རྩ་བའི་བླ་མ་བར། །
བྱིན་རླབས་དང་ནི་མན་ངག་ལ་སོགས་པའི། །
རྒྱུན་རྣམས་མ་ཆད་རིམ་པར་གཅིག་ནས་གཅིག །
ཡང་དག་བརྒྱུད་དེ་ཕྱོན་པའི་བླ་མའོ། །

གཉིས་པ་ནི།

།བླ་མས་བསྟན་པ་ཇི་བཞིན་རང་སེམས་ལ། །
ངེས་པ་སྐྱེས་ཤིང་དེ་ཉིད་རྒྱལ་བའི་བཀའ། །
གང་ལའང་འགལ་མེད་ཉམས་མྱོང་སྐྱེ་བའི་ཕྱིར། །
གསུངས་རབ་ཐམས་ཅད་གདམས་པར་འཆར་བས་སོ། །

གསུམ་པ་ནི།

འབྱུང་དང་འབྱུང་བ་ལས་གྱུར་ཕྱི་ནང་གི། །
འཁོར་འདས་དངོས་པོའི་ཆོས་རྣམས་ཐམས་ཅད་ཀྱིས། །
ལམ་གྱི་ཚུལ་རྣམས་བརྡ་དང་དཔེའི་སྒོ་ནས། །
སྟོན་ཕྱིར་དངོས་ཀུན་བླ་མར་མ་གྱུར་མེད། །

བཞི་པ་ནི།

དཔལ་ལྡན་བླ་མས་ཇི་ལྟར་ངོ་སྤྲོད་པའི། །
རང་སེམས་གནས་ལུགས་ཕྱིན་ཅི་མ་ལོག་པར། །
མངོན་སུམ་མཐོང་རྟོགས་གཏན་ལ་ཕེབས་པ་དེས། །
ཆོས་རྣམས་ཀུན་གྱི་དེ་བཞིན་ཉིད་ཀྱང་རྟོགས། །

གསུམ་པ་དམིགས་རྐྱེན་ནི།

ཕྱི་ནང་གྲུབ་མཐའི་བློ་ཡིས་མ་བསྒྱུར་ཅིང་། །
རྟོགས་པས་མ་བསླད་གདོད་མའི་གནས་ལུགས་ཀྱི། །

སེམས་ཀྱི་ངོ་བོ་སྐུ་གསུམ་གྱི་རོལ་པ། །
དེ་ཉིད་ཁོ་ན་ཉམས་སུ་བླང་བྱའོ། །

བཞི་པ་དེ་མ་ཐག་རྐྱེན་ནི།
དངོས་གཞི་ཉམས་སུ་ལེན་པའི་གནས་སྐབས་སུ། །
བསྒོམ་བྱ་སྒོམ་བྱེད་རྣམ་པར་མི་རྟོག་ཅིང་། །
སྤང་བླང་རེ་དོགས་བཟོ་བཅོས་མ་བྱས་པའི། །
ཐ་མལ་ཤེས་པའི་ངོ་བོ་ཁོ་ནར་སྐྱོངས། །

གཉིས་པ་དངོས་གཞི་ལ། ཞི་གནས་དང་། ལྷག་མཐོང་གཉིས། དང་པོ་ལའང་སྤྱི་དང་བྱེ་བྲག་གོ །དང་པོ་ལ་ལུས་གནད་དང་སེམས་གནད་གཉིས་ལས།

དང་པོ་ནི།
ལུས་གནད་རྣམ་པར་སྣང་མཛད་ཆོས་བདུན་ཏེ། །
རྐང་པ་རྡོར་སྐྱིལ་ལག་པ་མཉམ་པར་བཞག། །
དཔུང་པ་རྒོད་གཤོག་ལྟར་བརྒྱང་མགྲིན་པ་ནི། །
ལྕགས་ཀྱུ་ལྟར་དགུག་སྒལ་ཚིགས་མདའ་ལྟར་བསྲང་། །

མིག་ནི་སྣ་རྩེའི་སོར་བཞིའི་ནམ་མཁར་གཏད། །
མཆུ་དང་སོ་ནི་རང་བབས་བཞག་ཅིང་ལྕེ། །
ཡ་རྐན་ལ་སྦྱར་བདེ་བའི་སྟན་ལ་འཁོད། །

གཉིས་པ་ནི།
སེམས་ཀྱི་གནད་ནི་དེ་ཡང་ཇི་སྐད་དུ། །
མི་མནོ་མི་བསམ་མི་སེམས་མི་སྒོམ་ཞིང་། །
མི་དཔྱད་རང་སོར་བཞག་ཅེས་གསུངས་པ་བཞིན། །
དགག་སྒྲུབ་སྤང་བླང་རེ་དོགས་དངོས་འཛིན་གྱི། །

ཨ་འཐས་ཞེན་པ་དང་བྲལ་ཐ་མལ་གྱི། །
ཤེས་པ་སྐད་ཅིག་མ་འདིའི་ངོ་བོ་རུ། །

སྣོད་ཀྱི་སྙོད་ལ་མ་ཡེངས་རྩེ་གཅིག་ཏུ།།
གསལ་སྟོང་འཛིན་མེད་མ་བཅོས་ལྷུག་པར་ཞོག །

གཉིས་པ་བྱེ་བྲག་ལ། སེམས་པ་མ་ཟིན་པ་ཟིན་པར་བྱེད་པ། ཟིན་པ་བརྟན་པར་བྱེད་པ། བརྟན་པ་བོགས་དབྱུང་བ་བཅས་ལས། དང་པོ་ལ། དམིགས་པ་དང་བཅས་ཏེ་སེམས་འཛིན་པ། རླུང་ལ་སེམས་འཛིན་པའོ། །དང་པོ་ལ། ཕྱིར་འཛིན་པ་དང་ནང་དུ་འཛིན་པ་གཉིས། དང་པོ་ལ་མ་དག་པ་ལ་སེམས་འཛིན་པ་དང་། དག་པ་ལ་སེམས་འཛིན་པའོ།

དང་པོ་ནི།
ལྷ་སྣངས་ལུས་གནད་ལེགས་པར་བཅས་ཏེ་འཁོད།།
མདུན་གྱི་གཞི་ཙ་ཀ་བ་རྩིག་པ་སོགས།།
རག་པའི་གཟུགས་གང་ཞིག་ལ་གཏད་པ་ལས།།
གཞན་དུ་མ་ཡེངས་རྩེ་གཅིག་མཉམ་པར་བཞག །

དེ་བཞིན་མདུན་དུ་ཤིང་བུའམ་རྡེའུ་སྟེ།།
ཕྲ་བའི་གཟུགས་ལ་མ་ཡེངས་སེམས་འཛིན་ཞིང་།།
གཞན་ཡང་མར་མེ་ནམ་མཁའ་དེ་བཞིན་དུ།།
སྨིན་མཚམས་ཐིག་ལེ་དཀར་པོ་སྲན་མ་ཙམ།།
དམིགས་པའི་རྟེན་དུ་བྱས་ལ་སེམས་འཛིན་ནོ།།

གཉིས་པ་དག་པ་ལ་སེམས་འཛིན་པ་ནི།
མདུན་དུ་རྫོགས་པའི་སངས་རྒྱས་བཅོམ་ལྡན་འདས།།
སྐུ་མདོག་ཆ་ལུགས་མཚན་དང་དཔེ་བྱད་སོགས།།
ལེགས་པར་གསལ་བཏབ་དད་གུས་དང་བཅས་ཏེ།།
དེ་ལ་རྩེ་གཅིག་གཏད་དེ་སེམས་གཟུང་བྱ།།

གཉིས་པ་ནང་དུ་སེམས་འཛིན་པ་ནི།
རང་གི་སྙིང་གར་པད་འདབ་བརྒྱད་པའི་ལྟེར།།
ཡི་དམ་གང་རུང་བསྐྱེད་དམ་བླ་མ་སྒོམ།།
ཡང་ན་དེ་དག་གི་ནི་ངོ་བོ་རུ།།
འོད་ཀྱི་གོང་བུར་གསལ་ལ་སེམས་གཟུང་ངོ་།།

དེ་ལྟར་དམིགས་རྟེན་རྣམས་ལ་མ་ཡེངས་པར། །
ལྟ་སྟངས་དང་བཅས་གྲིམས་ལྷོད་སྐྱོན་དང་བྲལ། །
དྲན་པའི་རྒྱང་སོ་ཙམ་ལས་བཟོ་མེད་དང་། །
སྤང་བླང་རེ་དོགས་མེད་པར་རང་བབས་སུ། །
ལྷོད་ཀྱི་སྐྱོད་ལ་འགོལ་ལེ་ཤིག་གེར་ཞོག །

གཉིས་པ་དམིགས་པ་མེད་པ་ལ་སེམས་འཛིན་པ་ནི།

ཕྱི་ནང་དངོས་པོའི་ཆོས་རྣམས་ཐམས་ཅད་ཀུན། །
སྟོང་ཆེན་གཅིག་ཅར་པ་ལ་སེམས་འཛིན་པའམ། །
ཡང་ན་དེ་རྣམས་གཅིག་ལ་གཅིག་ཐིམ་ཞིང་། །
སྟོང་ཆེན་འོད་གསལ་བ་ལ་མཉམ་པར་བཞག །

གསུམ་པ་རླུང་ལ་སེམས་འཛིན་པ་ནི།

རླུང་ལ་སེམས་འཛིན་པ་ནི་བུམ་ཅན་ལ། །
གཏད་དམ་འབྱུང་འཇུག་གནས་གསུམ་གཅིག་རྩིས་པའི། །
ཉེར་གཅིག་ལ་སོགས་གྲངས་བཟུང་མ་ཡེངས་པར། །
གསལ་དངས་ངར་བཅས་ཡུན་ཐུང་གྲངས་མང་འབད། །

དེ་ལྟར་མན་ངག་རྣམས་ནི་སྒོམ་པའི་མཐུས། །
གནས་པ་གསུམ་ལས་དང་པོ་རི་གཟར་གྱི། །
ཁ་ནས་ཆུ་འབབས་དང་མཚུངས་གཉིས་པ་ནི། །
ཆུ་ཀླུང་དལ་འབབས་ཐ་མ་མི་གཡོ་བ། །
རྒྱ་མཚོ་ལྟ་བུ་རིམ་གྱིས་འཆར་བར་འགྱུར། །

གཉིས་པ་ཟིན་པ་བརྟན་པར་བྱེད་པ་ལ། སེམས་བཅིང་བ་དང་། སེམས་གནས་པར་བྱེད་པའི་ཐབས་དགུའོ། དང་པོ་ལ། སྙིང་དུ་བཅིང་བ་དང་། འོག་ཏུ་བཅིང་བ། སྦྱིལ་མའི་རྣལ་འབྱོར་རོ།

དང་པོ་ནི།

སྙིང་གར་པད་འདབ་བཞི་པའི་ལྟེ་བ་རུ། །
ཐིག་ལེ་དཀར་པོ་སྲན་མ་ཙམ་ཞིག་ལ། །

སེམས་འཛིན་རླུང་བཟུང་རླུང་ནི་ཕྱིར་གཏོང་མཉམ།།
ཐིག་ལེ་ཚངས་བུག་ནས་སོང་ནམ་མཁའི་དབྱིངས།།
གནས་པར་བསམ་ལ་ལུས་གནད་ལྟ་སྟངས་ནི།།
སྙིང་དུ་གཏུན་ལ་སེམས་ནི་གཟེངས་སྟོད་ཅིང་།།
རིག་པ་ཧུར་བཏོན་ཡུན་རིང་བསྒོམ་པར་བྱ།།

གཉིས་པ་ནི།
བཅིང་པ་བར་མ་རང་གི་སྙིང་ག་རུ།།
པདྨ་ནག་པོ་འདབ་བཞི་ཁ་འོག་ཏུ།།
མངོན་པར་ཕྱོགས་པའི་ལྟེ་བར་ཐིག་ལེ་ནག།
སྲན་མ་ཙམ་ཞིག་བ་ཐག་བཞིན་འཁྲིལ་ནས།།

གསང་བ་ནས་ཐོན་དལ་བུས་འོག་ཕྱོགས་སུ།།
དཔག་ཚད་དུ་མར་ལྕི་བའི་རྣམ་པ་ཡིས།།
གནས་པར་རྩེ་གཅིག་སེམས་བཟུང་སྲིན་ཞལ་བསྡམ།།
ལུས་གནད་ལྟ་སྟངས་ཐུར་དུ་དབབ་སྟེ་སྒོམ།།

གསུམ་པ་ནི།
གཞན་ཡང་ཚོད་དང་བསྟུན་ཏེ་སེམས་མཐོ་ན།།
སྨད་དང་དེ་བཞིན་དམའ་ན་སྟོད་པ་ཡི།།
དམིགས་པ་གཉིས་པོ་སྤེལ་མའི་རྣལ་འབྱོར་ལ།།
རྟག་ཏུ་ཆུ་བོའི་རྒྱུན་བཞིན་བསྟེན་པར་བྱ།།

གཉིས་པ་སེམས་གནས་པའི་ཐབས་དགུ་ནི།
འཛོག་དང་ཀུན་འཛོག་ངེས་པར་འཛོག་པ་དང་།།
ཉེར་འཛོག་དུལ་བར་བྱེད་དང་ཞི་བར་བྱེད།།
ཉེ་བར་ཞི་བྱེད་རྒྱུད་གཅིག་བྱེད་མཉམ་འཛོག།
འདི་དག་དོན་ནི་རིམ་པ་བཞིན་དུ་བསྟན།།

དམིགས་པ་གང་ལ་རྩེ་གཅིག་གཏད་དེ་འཛོག།
དེ་ཉིད་ཡུན་རིང་དུ་ནི་གནས་པར་བྱེད།།

གལ་ཏེ་རྣམ་རྟོག་འཕྲོ་ན་དེ་མ་ཐག །
དྲན་པས་བཟུང་སྟེ་མཉམ་པར་འཇོག་པའོ། །

མཉམ་པར་བཞག་པའི་སེམས་དེའང་སྔར་གྱི་ནི། །
གནས་པའི་སྟེང་དེར་བསྲེས་ཏེ་མཉམ་པར་འཇོག །
སེམས་གནས་དེ་ཡི་ཡོན་ཏན་རྣམས་དྲན་པས། །
དགའ་བ་བསྐྱེད་དེ་དེ་ཡི་ནང་དུ་གནས། །

གང་ལ་འཕྲོ་བའི་རྐྱེན་དེའོ་ཞེས། །
ངེས་ཤིང་དེ་ལ་ཞེན་པ་བཟློག་ཏེ་གནས། །
རྣམ་གཡེང་རྒྱུ་དང་ཡིད་མི་བདེ་བ་སོགས། །
ངོ་བོ་ངོས་བཟུང་རང་གྲོལ་ཉིད་དུ་བྱ། །

དེ་ལྟར་བསྒོམས་པས་ཤུགས་ཀྱི་དམིགས་པ་ལ། །
འཇུག་ཅིང་རྩོལ་བར་མི་ལྟོས་གནས་པར་ནུས། །
མཐར་ནི་མཉམ་པར་བཞག་དང་མ་བཞག་པའི། །
རྣམ་པར་གཡེང་བ་ཀུན་དང་བྲལ་བའོ། །

གསུམ་པ་བརྟན་པ་ཐོགས་དབྱུང་བ་ནི།
མིག་གི་ཡུལ་དུ་སྣང་བའི་གཟུགས་རྣམས་ལ། །
ཤེས་པ་གཏད་ཅིང་དེ་བཞིན་སྒྲ་སོགས་ལའང་། །
རིམ་གྱིས་དམིགས་རྟེན་བྱས་ནས་རྩེ་གཅིག་བཞག །
དེ་ཡང་རྣམ་པར་རྟོག་པ་གང་སྐྱེས་ཀྱང་། །

སྐྱོན་དུ་མི་བལྟ་དེ་ཐོག་ཅེན་གྱིས་བཞག །
སྒྲིམས་ལྷོད་གཉིས་སྤེལ་ཁྲིད་པར་གེགས་སེལ་དང་། །
བོགས་འདོན་མཆོག་གྱུར་བླ་མར་གསོལ་འདེབས་དང་། །
མུས་གུས་སྒོ་ནས་ཐུགས་ཡིད་གཅིག་ཏུ་བསྲེས། །

གཉིས་པ་ལྷག་མཐོང་ལ། གནས་ལུགས་སེམས་ཀྱི་ངོ་བོ་ལ་བལྟ་བ་དང་། གཞི་རྩ་གཅད་པ། རིག་སྟོང་དུ་གཏན་ལ་ཕབ་ནས་ངོ་སྤྲོད་པའོ།

དང་པོ་ནི།
།གནས་ལུགས་སེམས་ཀྱི་ངོ་བོར་བལྟ་བའི་ཚུལ། །
རང་བབས་མ་བཅོས་ལྷོད་ཀྱི་གློད་ནས་འཇོག །
ངོ་བོ་ཁ་དོག་གཟུགས་དབྱིབས་སོགས་ཇི་ལྟར། །
གཞིག་ཅིང་དཔྱོད་ལ་ཡང་ནས་ཡང་དུ་ལྟོས། །

གནས་པ་དེ་ཡི་ངོ་བོ་ཇི་ལྟར་ན། །
གསལ་ཞིང་ཧྲིག་གེ་བ་ལ་རྗེན་ནེར་དགོས། །
གལ་ཏེ་གནས་པ་བཙལ་བས་མ་རྙེད་ན། །
འཕྲོ་རུ་བཅུག་ལ་ཇི་ལྟར་འཕྲོ་ཞིང་དཔྱོད། །

གཉིས་པ་ནི།
།དེ་ནས་གཞི་རྩ་བཅད་པའི་ཚུལ་བསྟན་པར། །
བཙལ་ཚེ་མ་རྙེད་པ་ན་འཚོལ་མཁན་དང་། །
སེམས་དེའི་འབྱུང་གནས་འགྲོ་གསུམ་སོགས་ཇི་ལྟར། །
ལེགས་པར་བརྟག་ནས་ཡང་ཡང་བཙལ་བར་བྱ། །

གཞན་ཡང་ཡིད་ལ་བྱེད་པ་བཅུ་གཅིག་སྟེ། །
ཡོངས་ཚོལ་རབ་བྱེད་པ་དང་སོ་སོར་བརྟག །
ཞིབ་མོར་དཔྱོད་པ་ཞི་གནས་ལྷག་མཐོང་དང་། །
ཟུང་འབྲེལ་གསལ་བ་མི་རྟོག་བཏང་སྙོམ་དང་། །

རྒྱུན་མི་ཆད་པ་ཡེངས་པ་མེད་རབ་བྱེད། །
འདི་རྣམས་དོན་ནི་རིམ་པ་བཞིན་བསྟན་ཏེ། །
སེམས་ནི་ཡོད་མེད་ངོ་བོ་ཇི་ལྟར་ཞེས། །
སེམས་ཀྱི་རྒྱུད་ལ་བྲེང་ཆགས་སུ་ནི་བཙལ། །

ཁྱད་པར་ཁ་དོག་དང་ནི་དབྱིབས་ལ་སོགས། །
བྱུང་གནས་འགྲོ་གསུམ་གཞི་རྟེན་རྩད་གཅོད་དེ། །
ཚོལ་པོ་ཚོལ་མཁན་མཐར་ནི་ཐུག་པར་བཙལ། །
བཙལ་བས་རང་སེམས་རང་བཞིན་མེད་རྟོགས་པས། །

ཆོས་ཀུན་གནས་ལུགས་ཀྱང་ནི་གཏན་ཕེབས་ཕྱིར། །
ཟབ་མོའི་དོན་ལ་སེམས་ནི་ཉེ་བར་གནས། །
གནས་པ་དེ་ཉིད་ངོ་བོ་སྤྲ་མ་ལྟར། །
བཙལ་བའི་རང་ངོ་ཡོངས་སུ་རྟོགས་པའོ། །

དེ་དག་ཐ་དད་མ་ཡིན་དབྱེར་མི་ཕྱེད། །
གལ་ཏེ་བྱིང་ཞིང་རྒྱུགས་པར་གྱུར་པ་ན། །
རྒོད་རྒྱུ་ཡིན་ལ་བྱ་ཞིང་སེམས་གཟེངས་སྟོད། །
འཕྲོ་རྒོད་གྱུར་ན་ཞི་བའི་ཐབས་ལ་འབད། །

བྱིང་རྒོད་བྲལ་བར་གྱུར་པའི་གནས་སྐབས་སུ། །
ཚོལ་བརྟག་དཔྱད་པའི་ངོ་བོར་གནས་པར་བྱ། །
དེ་ལྟའི་རྣལ་འབྱོར་ནམ་ཡང་མི་འབྲལ་བྱ། །
དེ་ལ་སེམས་ནི་ཉེ་བར་བསྒྲིམས་བྱས་ནས། །
རྣམ་པར་གཡེང་བས་གླགས་མི་རྙེད་པར་བྱ། །
དེ་ལྟར་ཡིད་བྱེད་བཅུ་གཅིག་སྔོ་ནས་ཀྱང་། །
གཞི་རྩ་གཅད་པའི་ཚུལ་ལ་ཡང་ཡང་འབད། །

གསུམ་པ་ནི།
རིག་སྟོང་གཏན་ལ་ཕབ་ནས་ངོ་སྤྲོད་ཚུལ། །
ཐོག་མར་སེམས་ནི་རང་ལུགས་སྐྱོད་ལ་ཞོག །
སྐྱོད་པའི་སེམས་ཀྱི་ངོ་བོར་རྗེན་ནེར་ལྟོས། །
མ་ཡེངས་ཙམ་གྱི་དྲན་པ་རྒྱུན་ཆགས་བསྟེན། །

རྣམ་རྟོག་གང་ཤར་ཆེད་དུ་སྤང་བླང་དང་། །
བཅས་བཅོས་གང་ཡང་མི་བྱེད་ཐ་མལ་གྱི། །
ཤེས་པ་སྐད་ཅིག་ངོས་བཟུང་དང་བྲལ་བའི། །
གསལ་སྟོང་ལྷང་ངེ་བ་ལ་རྫིག་གེར་ཞོག །

ཡང་ངོ་སྤྲོད་གདབ་ཚུལ་ལ། འགྱུ་ཐོག་ནས་ངོ་སྤྲོད་པ་དང་སྡང་ཐོག་ནས་ངོ་སྤྲོད་པ་གཉིས་ལས།
དང་པོ་ནི།

གཞན་ཡང་འགྱུ་ཐོག་ནས་ནི་ངོ་སྤྲོད་ཚུལ། །
ཐོག་མར་ཤེས་པ་རང་ལུགས་སྐྱོད་ནས་བཞག །
དེ་ཡི་ངང་ནས་རང་གི་ངོ་བོ་བལྟ། །
དེ་ནས་འགྱུར་བཙུག་སྣང་ཡང་འགྱུ་མཁན་སེམས། །

དེ་དང་གནས་པའི་སེམས་ལ་ཁྱད་པར་ཅི། །
འགྱུ་སེམས་དེ་དང་དེ་ལ་བལྟ་བའི་སེམས། །
ཁྱད་པར་བལྟ་བའི་འགྱུ་བ་རང་གྲོལ་འགྲོ། །
དེ་ཡི་ངང་དུ་མ་ཡེངས་རྩེ་གཅིག་ཞོག །

གཉིས་པ་སྣང་ཐོག་ནས་ངོ་སྤྲོད་པ་ལ། སྣང་བ་སེམས། སེམས་སྟོང་པ། སྟོང་པ་ལྷུན་གྲུབ། ལྷུན་གྲུབ་རང་གྲོལ་དུ་ངོ་སྤྲོད་པ་རྣམས་ལས།

དང་པོ་ནི།
།གཟུགས་སོགས་དམིགས་པའི་རྟེན་བྱས་དེ་དང་སེམས། །
གཅིག་གམ་ཐ་དད་བརྟག་པས་ཕྱི་རོལ་གྱི། །
སྣང་བའི་ཡུལ་ཀུན་སེམས་ཀྱི་རང་མདངས་ལས། །
གཞན་དུ་གྲུབ་པ་མེད་པར་རྟོགས་གྱུར་ན། །
དེ་ཡི་ངང་དུ་འཛིན་མེད་ཕྲུད་དེ་ཞོག །

གཉིས་པ་སེམས་སྟོང་པར་ངོ་སྤྲོད་པ་ནི།
སེམས་ཉིད་ཅིར་ཡང་མ་གྲུབ་སྟོང་པ་ཉིད། །
དེ་ནི་གང་གིས་ཀྱང་ནི་མཚོན་དུ་མེད། །
སྨྲ་བསམ་བརྗོད་བྲལ་ནམ་མཁའ་ལྟ་བུ་སྟེ། །
དེ་ཡི་ངང་དུ་མ་མཙོས་ལྷུག་པར་ཞོག །

གསུམ་པ་སྟོང་པ་ལྷུན་གྲུབ་ཏུ་ངོ་སྤྲོད་པ་ནི།
སྟོང་པའི་ཆོས་ལས་གཡོ་བ་མེད་བཞིན་དུ། །
རྩལ་གདངས་མ་འགག་སྣ་ཚོགས་འཆར་བ་ཉིད། །
སྟོང་ལས་གཞན་མེད་སྣང་སྲིད་འཁོར་འདས་ཆོས། །
ལྷུན་གྲུབ་སྣང་སྟོང་དབྱེར་མེད་ཉིད་རིག་བྱ། །

བཞི་པ་ལྷུན་གྲུབ་རང་གྲོལ་དུ་ངོ་སྤྲོད་པ་ནི།
དེ་བཞིན་སྣང་རིག་སྟོང་གསུམ་གདོད་མ་ནས། །
གསལ་སྟོང་ཟུང་འཇུག་ལྷུན་གྱིས་གྲུབ་པ་ལ། །
སྤང་བླང་གསལ་བཞག་གཉེན་པོར་མ་ལྟོས་པར། །
དོན་གྱི་རང་གྲོལ་ཕྱག་རྒྱ་ཆེན་པོའོ། །

གསུམ་པ་རྗེས་ཀྱི་དོན་ལ། རང་གི་ངོ་བོ་བླ་མས་ངོ་སྤྲོད་པ། དེ་ཉམས་སུ་སྐྱོང་ནས་རྩལ་སྦྱངས་ཤིང་བོགས་འདོན་པའི་ཚུལ་དང་། གེགས་བསལ་བ། ལམ་འགྲོད་ཚུལ། འབྲས་བུ་མངོན་དུ་བྱེད་ཚུལ་དང་བཞི་ལས། དང་པོ་ལོག་རྟོག་ལྔ་བསལ་ཏེ་བོགས་འདོན་པ་ལས།

དང་པོ་ཡུལ་ལ་ལོག་རྟོག་བསལ་ཚུལ་ནི།
འཁོར་བ་སྤང་བྱ་མྱ་ངན་འདས་བསྒྲུབ་བྱར། །
ཨ་མཐས་ཞེན་འཛིན་མེད་པར་དགེ་སྡིག་སོགས། །
གཉིས་བསྡུས་ཆོས་ཀུན་གཉིས་མེད་ཡེ་ཤེས་དབྱིངས། །
རོ་མཉམ་བྱས་པས་ཡུལ་ལ་ལོག་རྟོག་སེལ། །

གཉིས་པ་དུས་ལ་ལོག་རྟོག་བསལ་ཚུལ་ནི།
དུས་གསུམ་བདེན་དངོས་གྲུབ་པ་མེད་བཞིན་དུ། །
དུས་གསུམ་དབྱེ་བ་རྫོངས་པས་བཏགས་པ་སྟེ། །
དེ་ཕྱིར་དུས་གསུམ་ཐ་དད་མ་གྲུབ་པར། །
མཉམ་ཉིད་རྟོགས་པ་དུས་ལ་ལོག་རྟོག་སེལ། །

གསུམ་པ་ངོ་བོ་ལ་ལོག་རྟོག་བསལ་ཚུལ་ནི།
ད་ལྟའི་སེམས་འདི་སྤང་ནས་ཕྱིས་ཡེ་ཤེས། །
ཐོབ་པར་འདོད་པ་ཕྱིན་ཅི་ལོག་པ་སྟེ། །
རང་སེམས་གདོད་ནས་ཡེ་ཤེས་ལྷུའི་རང་བཞིན། །
ཡིན་པར་ཤེས་པ་ངོ་བོར་ལོག་རྟོག་སེལ། །

བཞི་པ་རང་བཞིན་ལ་ལོག་རྟོག་བསལ་ཚུལ་ནི།
སེམས་ཅན་རྣམས་ཀྱི་ཕུང་ཁམས་སྐྱེ་མཆེད་ཀུན། །
གདོད་ནས་དེ་བཞིན་གཤེགས་པ་གཤེགས་མ་དང་། །

ལྷ་དང་ལྷ་མོའི་རང་བཞིན་ཉིད་གནས་པ། །
དེ་ལྟར་ཤེས་པ་རང་བཞིན་ཡོག་རྟོག་སེལ། །

ལྔ་པ་ཤེས་རབ་ལ་ཡོག་རྟོག་བསལ་ཚུལ་ནི།

དམ་པའི་དོན་ནི་ཤེས་རབ་ཆེ་བ་དང་། །
རྟོག་གེའི་ཡུལ་མིན་བླ་མའི་བྱིན་རླབས་དང་། །
སྐལ་ལྡན་ལས་འཕྲོ་ཅན་གྱིས་རྟོགས་པ་སྟེ། །
དེ་ནི་ཤེས་རབ་ལ་ནི་ཡོག་རྟོག་སེལ། །

གཉིས་པ་མཁས་པ་གསུམ་ལ་སློབ་པ་སྟེ། དང་པོ་སྒོམ་གྱི་མགོ་རྩོམ་པ་ལ་མཁས་པ། བར་དུ་སྒོམ་གྱི་འཕྲོ་གཅོད་པ་ལ་མཁས་པ། མཐར་ཉམས་བསྐྱང་བ་ལ་མཁས་པ་དང་བཅས་སོ།

དང་པོ་ནི།

ལུས་གནད་ལེགས་བཅས་འགྲོ་ན་འགྲོ་ཐོག་དང་། །
གནས་ན་གནས་ཐོག་ངོ་བོ་ལ་བལྟས་ཏེ། །
མ་བཅོས་སོ་མ་ལྷུག་པ་རང་བབས་ངང་། །
མ་ཡེངས་རང་ངོ་ཤེས་ཙམ་ཐོག་ཏུ་ཞོག །

གཉིས་པ་ནི།

གང་ལ་མཉམ་བཞག་རྒྱུན་རིང་གཙོར་མི་འདོན། །
ཏིང་ངེ་འཛིན་དང་ལུས་གནད་རྣམས་བསྒྱུར་ཞིང་། །
ཡུན་ཐུང་གྲངས་མང་གསལ་དངས་ངར་བཅས་ཏེ། །
སྒོམ་དང་འཕོན་གྱིས་མ་སོང་བྲོད་པ་བསྐྱེད། །

གསུམ་པ་ནི།

།བདེ་གསལ་མི་རྟོག་ཉམས་གསུམ་གང་ཤར་ཡང་། །
ཆགས་ཞེན་ང་རྒྱལ་སྐྱེས་ན་ཉམས་ཀྱི་ཕྱིར། །
རྟོགས་པ་ཤོར་བ་ཞེས་བྱ་དེ་བས་ནི། །
ཉམས་ལ་ཞེན་པ་བྲལ་བའི་ངང་ནས་སྐྱོངས། །

གསུམ་པ་ཤོར་ས་དང་གོལ་ས་བཅད་དེ་ཐོགས་འདོན་པ་ནི། དང་པོ་ཤོར་ས་ལ། སྟོང་ཉིད་ཤེས་བྱའི་གཤིས་ལ་ཤོར་བ་དང་། རྒྱས་འདེབས་སུ་ཤོར་བ། གཉེན་པོར་ཤོར་བ། ལམ་དུ་ཤོར་བ་དང་བཞི་ལས།

དང་པོ་ནི།

།ཕྱུང་རིག་ཐོས་བསམ་ཐ་སྙད་ཀྱི་སྒོ་ནས། །
དངོས་པོའི་གནས་ལུགས་སྟོང་པ་གཏན་ཐབ་ཅིང་། །
ཐམས་ཅད་སྟོང་པས་སྒོམ་རྒྱུ་ཅི་ཡོད་ཅེས། །
བློས་བྱས་སྒོ་ནས་འཛོག་ཕྱིར་ཡང་དག་མིན། །

གཉིས་པ་ནི།

སྟོང་ཉིད་རྒྱས་འདེབས་ཤོར་ཞེས་དངོས་པོ་ཀུན། །
སྟོང་ཉིད་མ་ཡིན་པར་བཟུང་ཤུཙྪ་ཏའི། །
སྔགས་སོགས་བརྗོད་པས་སྟོང་པར་སོང་སྙམ་ཏེ། །
སྒོམ་པར་བྱེད་པའང་ཡང་དག་མ་ཡིན་ནོ། །

གསུམ་པ་ནི།

སྟོང་ཉིད་གཉེན་པོར་ཤོར་ཞེས་དུག་གསུམ་སོགས། །
རྣམ་རྟོག་སྐྱེས་ཚེ་འདི་རྣམས་སྟོང་ཉིད་ཀྱིས། །
གཞོམ་པར་བྱའོ་སྙམ་སྟེ་སྟོང་ཉིད་དུ། །
མཉམ་པར་འཇོག་པ་དེ་ནི་དྲི་མ་ཅན། །

བཞི་པ་ནི།

སྟོང་ཉིད་ལམ་དུ་ཤོར་ཞེས་སྟོང་ཉིད་ལ། །
ལམ་དང་འབྲས་བུ་གཉིས་སུ་མེད་བཞིན་དུ། །
ད་ལྟ་སྟོང་ཉིད་སྒོམ་པ་དེས་ལམ་བྱས། །
ཕྱི་ནས་འབྲས་བུ་ཐོབ་སྙམ་ཡང་དག་མིན། །

གཉིས་པ་སྒོམ་པའི་གོལ་ས་བཅད་དེ་ཐོགས་འདོན་པ་ནི།

དེ་བཞིན་གོལ་ས་བཅད་དེ་ཐོགས་འདོན་ཚུལ། །
རྣམ་གྲངས་བཅུ་བདུན་རིམ་བཞིན་བསྟན་པར་བྱ། །

བདེ་གསལ་མི་རྟོག་གསུམ་ལས་བདེ་ཉམས་ལ། །
ཟག་བཅས་ཟག་མེད་སོ་སོར་མ་ཕྱེ་བར། །

སྤྱིར་གྱི་བདེ་ལ་ཤེས་རབ་ཀྱིས་བརྟག་པ། །
དེ་ཉིད་བསྒོམས་ནས་ཡང་དག་ཞེན་གྱུར་ན། །
འདོད་པའི་ཁམས་སུ་གོལ་ཞིང་དེ་བཞིན་དུ། །
གསལ་བའི་ཉམས་ལ་ཞེན་ན་གཟུགས་ཁམས་གོལ། །

མི་རྟོག་པ་ལ་ཞེན་ན་གཟུགས་མེད་སྐྱེ། །
དེ་ལའང་ཆོས་ཀུན་ནམ་མཁའ་དང་འདྲ་ཞེས། །
ཤེས་རབ་ཀྱིས་དཔྱད་ཡང་དག་ཞེན་གྱུར་ན། །
ནམ་མཁའ་མཐའ་ཡས་སྐྱེ་མཆེད་ཉིད་དུ་སྐྱེ། །

ཆོས་རྣམས་སེམས་ཡིན་སྙམ་དུ་བཟུང་བ་ལས། །
རྣམ་ཤེས་མཐའ་ཡས་སྐྱེ་མཆེད་ལ་ནི་གོལ། །
ཅི་ཡང་མ་གྲུབ་སྙམ་དུ་ཞེན་པས་ན། །
ཅི་ཡང་མེད་པའི་སྐྱེ་མཆེད་ཉིད་དུ་གོལ། །

ཡོད་མིན་མེད་མིན་སྙམ་དུ་ཞེན་གྱུར་ན། །
འདུ་ཤེས་མེད་མིན་སྐྱེ་མཆེད་ལ་ནི་སྐྱེ། །
དེས་ན་བདེ་གསལ་མི་རྟོག་ཉམས་རྣམས་ལ། །
ཆགས་ཞེན་དང་བྲལ་རང་ཞལ་མཐོང་བས་སེལ། །

ཐབས་དང་བྲལ་ཞིང་སྟོང་པར་ཞེན་གྱུར་ན། །
དམན་པར་གོལ་བས་དེ་ཉིད་སྟོང་པའི་ཚུལ། །
བརྩེ་བ་སྙིང་རྗེ་བྱང་ཆུབ་སེམས་བསྒོམ་བྱ། །
ཐབས་ཀྱིས་ཤེས་རབ་བོགས་འདོན་ཤེས་རབ་ཀྱིས། །

ཐབས་ཀྱི་བོགས་འདོན་དེ་གཉིས་ཟུང་འཇུག་གིས། །
གཅིག་གི་བོགས་འདོན་གཅིག་ཤོས་འདོན་པར་བྱ། །

ཞི་གནས་བོགས་ནི་ལྷག་མཐོང་གིས་འདོན་ཞིང་། །
ལྷག་མཐོང་བོགས་ཀྱང་ཞི་གནས་ཀྱིས་འདོན་བྱ། །

ཞི་གནས་ལྷག་མཐོང་གཉིས་པོ་རྩེ་གཅིག་ལ། །
ཉམས་ཀྱི་བོགས་ནི་ཉམས་ཀྱིས་འདོན་པར་བྱ། །
དེ་བཞིན་སྤྲོས་བྲལ་ལ་ནི་རྟོགས་པའི་བོགས། །
ཉམས་ཀྱིས་འདོན་པར་བྱ་ཞིང་རོ་གཅིག་ལ། །

རྟོགས་པའི་བོགས་ནི་རྟོགས་པས་འདོན་པར་བྱ། །
སྒོ་གསུམ་ཐ་མལ་དུ་ནི་མ་ལུས་པར། །
ཅི་བྱེད་དགེ་བའི་ཡོ་ལང་ཉིད་བསྒྱུར་ནས། །
ཐ་མལ་ཡོན་ཏན་དུ་ནི་བོགས་འདོན་བྱ། །

ཉོན་མོངས་སྡུག་བསྔལ་བར་ཆད་ལ་སོགས་སྐྱོན། །
སྤང་བླང་མེད་པར་རང་ཞལ་ལ་བལྟས་ནས། །
ལྟས་ངན་གཡང་དུ་ལེན་ནས་བོགས་འདོན་ནོ།།

བཞི་པ་འཕྲང་གསུམ་བསྒྲལ་ཏེ་བོགས་འདོན་པ་ལ། སྟོང་པ་དགྲར་ལངས་དང་། སྙིང་རྗེ་དགྲར་ལངས་དང་། རྒྱུ་འབྲས་དགྲར་ལངས་དང་གསུམ་ལས།

དང་པོ་ནི།
སེམས་ཀྱི་ངོ་བོར་དཔྱད་ཅིང་བལྟས་པའི་ཚེ། །
ཅི་ཡང་མ་གྲུབ་མཐོང་བས་ཆོས་ཐམས་ཅད། །
སྟོང་ཉིད་ཁོ་ན་ཡིན་ཕྱིར་དགེ་སྡིག་དང་། །
རྒྱུ་འབྲས་སོགས་ཀྱང་གྲུབ་པ་མེད་སྙམ་སྟེ། །

སྤང་གཉེན་མི་བཟུང་ནག་པོ་ཁ་འཐྱམས་ཞེས། །
སྟོང་པ་དགྲར་ལངས་ཡིན་ཏེ་དུག་ལྟར་སྤོངས། །

གཉིས་པ་ནི།

བདག་ཉིད་ཏིང་འཛིན་བདེ་བ་ཅུང་ཟད་ཙམ། །
ཐོབ་པས་དེ་དང་མི་ལྡན་སེམས་ཅན་རྣམས། །
གྲོལ་བར་བྱ་སྙམ་རང་གི་ཏིང་ངེ་འཛིན། །
ངོར་ནས་རྩོལ་བ་དང་བཅས་འདུས་བྱས་ཀྱི། །

དགེ་ལ་འཇུག་ཅིང་བདེན་པར་ཞེན་པ་ནི། །
སྙིང་རྗེ་དཀར་ལངས་ཞེས་བྱ་དེ་སྤོང་སྟེ། །
སྙིང་རྗེ་སྐྱེས་པ་དེ་དང་འབྲལ་མེད་ངང་། །
རང་གི་རྟོགས་པ་དྲི་མེད་སྐྱོང་ལ་འབད། །

གསུམ་པ་ནི།

གནས་ལུགས་ཟབ་མོ་མཐོང་བར་བྱེད་པ་ལ། །
ཤེས་བྱ་ཀུན་ལ་མཁས་པར་དགོས་སྙམ་སྟེ། །
སྒྲ་ཚད་སོགས་ལ་འཇུག་ཅིང་ཞི་ལྷག་གི། །
རྣལ་འབྱོར་ངོར་བར་བྱེད་ན་རྒྱུ་འབྲས་ཀྱི། །

རྟོག་པ་དཀར་ལངས་ཞེས་བྱ་ཡང་དག་མིན། །
དེ་ཕྱིར་ཟབ་མོའི་དོན་ལ་རྩེ་གཅིག་ཏུ། །
བསྒོམས་པས་སྣང་སྲིད་འཁོར་འདས་ཆོས་ཀུན་ལ། །
རློངས་པ་མེད་པའི་དྲི་མེད་ཤེས་རབ་ཐོབ། །

གཉིས་པ་གེགས་སེལ་ལ། ནད་དང་གདོན་དང་། ཏིང་ངེ་འཛིན་གྱི་གེགས་སེལ་གསུམ་ལས།

དང་པོ་ནི།

ཞི་གནས་གཙོ་བོར་བསྒོམས་པས་རླུང་ནད་སེལ། །
ལྷག་མཐོང་བསྒོམས་པས་བད་འཁྲིས་ནད་དག་སེལ། །
ཡང་ན་ཚ་གྲང་ནད་གཉིས་ཞི་ལྷག་གིས། །
རིམ་གྱིས་སེལ་ཞིང་དེ་བཞིན་ནད་གང་གི །

ངོ་བོ་དབྱིབས་དང་བྱུང་གནས་འགྲོ་གསུམ་བརྟགས། །
ཁྱད་པར་གཏོང་ལེན་དམིགས་པར་ནན་ཏན་བྱ། །

ཡང་ན་ནད་ནི་སྐྱེ་མེད་ཆོས་ཀྱི་སྐུ། །
གནས་མེད་ལོང་སྐུ་འགག་པ་མེད་སྤྲུལ་སྐུ། །
རང་བཞིན་སྟོང་པ་ངོ་བོ་ཉིད་སྐུ་སྟེ། །
སྐུ་བཞིའི་རོལ་པར་ཁྱེར་ཏེ་རང་ཞལ་ལྟོས། །

གཉིས་པ་ནི།

དེ་བཞིན་གདོན་གྱི་གེགས་སེལ་ཚུལ་ལ་ཡང་། །
གདོན་དུ་སྣང་བ་སེམས་ཀྱི་ཆོ་འཕྲུལ་ཏེ། །
སེམས་ཉིད་སྐུ་བཞིར་ཁྱེར་ལ་གདོན་དེ་ཡང་། །
སྐུ་བཞིའི་ལམ་དུ་ཁྱེར་བའི་སྒོ་ནས་སེལ། །

གསུམ་པ་ནི།

སྤྱིར་ན་བྱིང་རྒོད་སྐྱོན་སེལ་སྔར་བསྟན་བཞིན། །
འདི་ན་བླ་མའི་རྣལ་འབྱོར་གྱིས་སེལ་ན། །
བྱིང་ཚེ་སྤྱི་བོར་བླ་མ་འོད་དཔག་མེད། །
དེ་ལ་བརྒྱུད་པའི་བླ་མ་སོགས་བསྐྱིམ་ལ། །

མོས་གུས་གསོལ་བཏབ་དེ་ལས་འོད་འཕྲོས་ནས། །
རང་ཐིམ་བྱིང་བའི་རྒྱུ་རྣམས་སིངས་ཀྱིས་དག །
བླ་མ་འོད་ཞུ་རང་ལ་ཐིམ་པ་ཡིས། །
རང་ལུས་འོད་ཀྱི་གོང་བུ་ཞིང་ཁམས་ཀུན། །

སྣང་བར་བྱེད་པ་དེ་ཉིད་ནམ་མཁར་དེངས། །
རིག་པ་ངར་དང་བཅས་ཏེ་ཡེ་རེར་ཞོག །
རྒོད་ན་བླ་མ་རྗེར་སེམས་སྐུ་མདོག་སྔོ། །
པད་འདབ་བཞི་ཡི་རྣམ་པ་ཅན་གྱི་སྙིང་། །

དབུས་སུ་བསྒོམ་ལ་འདབ་བཞིར་རྣམ་སྣང་སོགས། །
སྐུ་མདོག་དེ་དང་མཚུངས་ལ་རང་རང་གི །
རིགས་ཀྱི་དཔའ་བོ་ཧཱུ་ཀི་སོགས་ཀྱིས་བསྐོར། །
དེ་རྣམས་ཐུགས་ལས་འོད་ཟེར་སྔོན་པོ་འཕྲོས། །

ཧླ་མར་ཟུག་པས་ཕྱོགས་མཚམས་ཐམས་ཅད་དུ། །
འོད་ཟེར་གྱིས་ནི་བརྒྱངས་པར་གསལ་བཏབ་སྟེ། །
ཕྱག་ཆེན་ངང་དུ་མཉམ་པར་བཞག་པས་སེལ། །
གཞན་ཡང་ཡིད་ཀྱོད་གང་བྱུང་དེའི་ངོ་བོར། །
མ་ཡེངས་མི་སྒོམ་བཟོ་མེད་ལྷུག་པར་ཞོག

གསུམ་པ་ལམ་བགྲོད་ཚུལ་ནི། རྣལ་འབྱོར་བཞིའི་ཚུལ་གྱིས་ལམ་གོང་ནས་གོང་དུ་བགྲོད་ཚུལ་བསྟན་ཅིང་། དེ་རེ་རེ་ལའང་ཆུང་འབྲིང་ཆེ་གསུམ་དུ་དབྱེ་བས་བཅུ་གཉིས་སུ་འགྱུར་རོ།

དེ་ལས་དང་པོ་རྩེ་གཅིག་ནི།
ཐོག་མར་རྩེ་གཅིག་རྣལ་འབྱོར་ཞེས་བྱ་ནི། །
སེམས་ཀྱི་རང་ངོ་ཚུལ་བཞིན་ཤེས་པ་སྟེ། །
གསལ་སྟོང་མ་འགག་མཁའ་ལྟར་མཐའ་དབུས་མེད། །
དེ་ཡི་ངང་དུ་སིང་ངེ་ཡེ་རེ་གནས། །

དེ་ལ་ཆུང་འབྲིང་ཆེ་གསུམ་དབྱེ་བ་ལས། །
ཆུང་དུ་བདེ་གསལ་ངོ་བོ་མཐོང་བ་དང་། །
འབྲིང་པོ་ཉིང་ངེ་འཛིན་ལ་རང་དབང་ཐོབ། །
ཆེན་པོ་དེ་ཡི་ཉམས་ནི་འཕོར་ཡུག་སོང་། །

གཉིས་པ་སྤྲོས་བྲལ་ནི།
།སེམས་ཉིད་རྩ་བྲལ་རྟོགས་པ་སྤྲོས་བྲལ་ཏེ། །
གཟུང་འཛིན་ཆོས་ཀུན་སྐྱེ་འགག་གནས་གསུམ་དང་། །
མཚན་མར་འཛིན་པའི་སྤྲོས་པ་ལས་གྲོལ་ནས། །
སྐྱེ་མེད་སྟོང་པ་ཉིད་དུ་སྒྲོ་འདོགས་ཆོད། །

དེ་ཡི་ཆུང་ངུ་རང་སེམས་སྐྱེ་མེད་རྟོགས། །
འབྲིང་པོ་སྣང་འཛིན་སྟོང་འཛིན་གཞི་རྩ་བྲལ། །
ཆེན་པོ་ཆོས་ཀུན་སྤྲོས་པའི་སྒྲོ་འདོགས་ཆོད། །

གསུམ་པ་རོ་གཅིག་ནི།
།སྣང་སེམས་འདྲེས་པ་རོ་གཅིག་རྣལ་འབྱོར་ཏེ། །
སྣང་སྲིད་འཁོར་འདས་ཆོས་ལ་སྐྱེ་འགག་གི། །
སྤྲོས་པ་བྲལ་དང་མ་བྲལ་སྟོང་མི་སྟོང་། །
དགག་སྒྲུབ་སྤང་བླང་མེད་པར་གཉུག་མའི་ངང་། །

མཉམ་པ་ཉིད་གྱུར་དེ་ཡི་ཆུང་ངུ་ནི། །
གཉིས་བསྡུས་ཆོས་རྣམས་གཅིག་ཏུ་རོ་མཉམ་འདྲེས། །
འབྲིང་པོ་སྣང་སེམས་ཆུ་ལ་ཆུ་བཞག་བཞིན། །
ཆེན་པོ་ཆོས་ཀུན་མཉམ་ཉིད་ངང་དུ་ཞི། །

བཞི་པ་སྒོམ་མེད་ནི།
སྔར་གྱི་ཉམས་དང་སྦྱོང་བ་དག་པའམ། །
བློ་ནི་གཏན་ཟད་སོང་བར་སྒོམ་མེད་ཡིན། །
དེ་ལ་ཆུང་ངུ་འབྲིང་དང་ཆེ་གསུམ་ལས། །
ཆུང་ངུ་བསྒོམ་བྱ་སྒོམ་བྱེད་ཀུན་དང་བྲལ། །

འབྲིང་པོ་ལྷུན་གྱིས་གྲུབ་པའི་རང་ས་ཟིན། །
ཆེན་པོ་འོད་གསལ་མ་བུ་འདྲེས་པ་ལས། །
ཆོས་དབྱིངས་ཡེ་ཤེས་ཀློང་དུ་འབྱམས་གྱུར་ཏེ། །
དོན་གཉིས་མཐར་ཕྱིན་རྫོགས་སངས་རྒྱས་པའོ། །

རྣལ་འབྱོར་བཞི་གསུམ་བཅུ་གཉིས་པོ་དེ་ལམ་དང་སྦྱར་ན།

རྣལ་འབྱོར་བཅུ་གཉིས་པོ་རྣམས་ཕར་ཕྱིན་གྱི། །
ས་དང་ལམ་ལ་གལ་ཏེ་སྦྱར་འདོད་ན། །

རྩེ་གཅིག་ཆུང་ངུ་ཚོགས་ཀྱི་ལམ་དང་ནི། །
འབྲིང་པོ་སྦྱོར་ལམ་དྲོད་རྩེ་ཆེན་པོ་ནི། །

བཟོད་པ་ཆོས་མཆོག་ལ་སྦྱར་སྤྲོས་བྲལ་གྱི། །
ཆུང་ངུ་མཐོང་བའི་ལམ་དང་ས་དང་པོ། །
འབྲིང་པོ་ས་གཉིས་པ་ནས་ལྔ་པའི་བར། །
ཆེན་པོ་སྐབས་སུ་ས་ནི་དྲུག་པ་ཐོབ། །

རོ་གཅིག་ཆུང་ངུ་རྟོགས་པའི་ས་བདུན་པ། །
འབྲིང་པོ་ས་བརྒྱད་ཆེན་པོ་ས་དགུར་སྦྱར། །
སྒོམ་མེད་ཆུང་ངུ་ས་བཅུ་ལ་སྦྱར་ཞིང་། །
འབྲིང་པོ་རྒྱུན་མཐའི་ས་དང་ཆེན་པོ་ནི། །
མཐར་ཕྱིན་ལམ་དང་བཅུ་གཅིག་ས་ལ་སྦྱར། །

བཞི་པ་འབྲས་བུ་མངོན་དུ་བྱེད་ཚུལ་ནི།

དེ་ལྟར་རྣལ་འབྱོར་བཅུ་གཉིས་རིམ་བཞིན་དུ། །
རྒྱུད་ལ་སྐྱེས་ཏེ་སྒོམ་མེད་མཐར་ཕྱིན་པས། །
སྒྲིབ་གཉིས་བག་ཆགས་མ་ལུས་ཕྱིར་གཞིལ་ཅིང་། །
མཁྱེན་གཉིས་ཡེ་ཤེས་ལང་ཚོ་ཀུན་རྫོགས་ནས། །

རང་དོན་ཆོས་ཀྱི་སྐུ་ལས་མ་གཡོས་ཀྱང་། །
གཞན་དོན་གཟུགས་སྐུས་འཁོར་བ་མ་སྟོངས་བར། །
རྣམ་རྟོག་འབད་རྩོལ་སྤྲོས་པ་མི་མངའ་བཞིན། །
འགྲོ་དོན་མཛད་ལ་ཕྲིན་ལས་རྟག་པ་དང་། །
ཁྱབ་པའི་བདག་ཉིད་ལྷུན་གྱིས་གྲུབ་པའོ། །

སྨར་སྨྲས་པ།
འདིར་འབད་དགེ་བའི་དངོས་པོ་ཡིས། །
སྐྱེ་དང་ཚེ་རབས་དུས་རྟག་ཏུ། །

སྲིད་ལས་ངེས་འབྱུང་ཚུལ་གནས་ཤིང་། །
བསླབ་གཞི་ཕྲ་མོའང་མི་འགལ་ཤོག །

གཞན་ཕན་བྱང་ཆུབ་སེམས་མཆོག་གཉིས། །
རྨི་ལམ་དུ་ཡང་མི་བརྗེད་ཅིང་། །
བསྡུས་དངོས་བཞི་དང་ཕྱིན་དྲུག་གིས། །
འགྲོ་ཀུན་བདེ་ལ་འགོད་ནུས་ཤོག །

ཡང་དག་དགེ་བའི་བཤེས་གཉེན་རྣམས། །
སྲོག་ལྟར་གཅེས་པར་འཛིན་འགྱུར་ལ། །
མཉེས་པ་ཀུན་གྱིས་རབ་མཉེས་ནས། །
དད་དང་དམ་ཚིག་ལ་གནས་ཤོག །

དེ་ཡི་མཐུ་ལ་བརྟེན་ནས་ནི། །
སོ་ཐར་བྱང་ཆུབ་སེམས་དཔའ་དང་། །
རིག་འཛིན་སྔགས་ཀྱི་སྡེ་སྣོད་ཀུན། །
རང་དོན་ཐོས་དང་བསམ་སྒོམ་གསུམ། །

གཞན་དོན་འཆད་དང་རྩོད་རྩོམ་གསུམ། །
གཉིས་དོན་མཁས་དང་བཙུན་བཟང་གསུམ། །
བསྟན་དོན་འཛིན་དང་སྐྱོང་སྤེལ་གསུམ། །
དེ་ཀུན་མཐའ་རུ་ཕྱིན་པར་ཤོག །

ངེས་དོན་ཕྱིར་མི་ལྡོག་པའི་གཞུང་། །
ཁྱད་པར་གནས་ལུགས་ཕྱག་རྒྱ་ཆེ། །
ཚུལ་བཞིན་རྟོགས་ཏེ་གཞན་ལ་ཡང་། །
སྤེལ་བའི་བྱེད་པོ་ཉིད་གྱུར་ཅིག །

མདོར་ན་ནམ་མཁའི་མཐས་གཏུགས་པའི། །
ལུས་ཅན་མ་ལུས་བདག་ཕོ་ནས། །

ཡང་དག་རྫོགས་པའི་སངས་རྒྱས་ཀྱི། །
གོ་འཕང་མཆོག་ལ་འགོད་ནུས་ཤོག །

མཆོག་གསུམ་རྒྱལ་བའི་བྱིན་རླབས་དང་། །
ལྷག་བསམ་རྣམ་པར་དག་པའི་སྟོབས། །
སྟོང་དང་རྟེན་འབྱུང་ཟབ་མོའི་མཐུས། །
སྨོན་པ་ཇི་བཞིན་འགྲུབ་གྱུར་ཅིག །

ཅེས་པ་འདི་ནི་རྗེ་ཞྭ་དམར་དྲུག་པ་ཆོས་ཀྱི་དབང་ཕྱུག་གིས་ཆོས་དྲུག་བདུད་རྩི་ཉིང་ཁུའི་ཁྲིད་ཡིག་གི་སྙིང་པོ་རྩ་ཚིག་སྒོམ་དོན་ཚིགས་བཅད་དུ་བསྡུས་པར་མཛད་པ་ཉམས་ལེན་སྐབས་སྒོམ་འདོན་ཤིན་ཏུ་སྟབས་བདེ་བས་ཕྱག་ཆེན་ལའང་དེ་ལྟ་བུ་ཞིག་བྱུང་ན་སྙམ་པའི་འདུན་པ་སྔར་ནས་ཡོད་མུས་ཐོག ད་ལམ་གནས་མདོ་སྐུ་ཆུང་མཆོག་སྤྲུལ་རིན་པོ་ཆེ་དང་དིལ་ཡག་བླ་མ་ཚེ་མཐར་གཉིས་ནས་ལོ་གསུམ་སྒྲུབ་པར་བཞུགས་པའི་སྐབས་གོང་གསལ་ཆོས་དྲུག་རྩ་ཚིག་དེ་ཉིད་ཟུར་དུ་པར་འདེབས་གནང་སྐབས་དེ་དང་ཆབས་ཅིག་ཕྱག་ཆེན་ལའང་འདི་ལྟར་དགོས་ཞེས་དོན་གཉེར་ཅན་འགས་བསྐུལ་ངོར། ཉམས་ལེན་གསར་བུ་བ་རྣམས་ལ་ཅུང་ཟད་ཕན་དུ་རེ་བའི་ལྷག་པའི་བསམ་པ་བཟང་པོས་ཉེ་བར་མཚམས་སྦྱར་ཏེ། ༄རྒྱལ་བའི་དབང་པོ་དཔལ་ཀརྨ་པའི་གདན་ས་ཆེན་པོ་འོག་མིན་བཤད་སྒྲུབ་ཆོས་འཁོར་གླིང་གི་སྒྲུབ་སྡེ་ཆེན་པོ་ཡིད་འོང་བསམ་གཏན་གླིང་གི་སྒྲུབ་དཔོན་བླ་མའི་མིང་འཛིན་འབོ་དཀར་སྤྲུལ་སྐུ་ཀརྨ་ངེས་དོན་ཆོས་ཀྱི་བློ་གྲོས་ཀྱིས་རྗོར་གླིང་། མི་རིགས་ཞེས་པ་སྨན་ལྗོངས་ཞི་བའི་བསྟི་གནས་འབོ་དཀར་ངེས་དོན་ཆོས་འཁོར་གླིང་དུ་ཕྱི་ལོ་ ༡༩༩༨ ཕྱི་ཟླ་ ༡༢ པའི་ཚེས་ ༡༣ ཞིང་བོད་ཟླ་ ༡༠ པའི་ཚེས་ ༢༠ ཕུར་རྒྱལ་མི་ཆུང་འགྲུབ་སྦྱོར་དང་ལྡན་པའི་དུས་ཚེས་ཉིན་བྲིས་པ་དགེ་ལེགས་འཕེལ།། །།

About the Author

Zurmang Gharwang Rinpoche was born on June 30, 1965, and prior to his birth he was recognized by His Holiness the sixteenth Gyalwa Karmapa as the twelfth incarnation of the Gharwang Tulku. He is the supreme lineage holder of the Zurmang Ear-Whispered Lineage (*Zur mang snyan rgyud*).

The unbroken line of the Gharwang Tulkus begins in the fourteenth century with the great siddha Trung Mase, the first Gharwang Tulku and founder of the Zurmang Kagyu tradition and Zurmang Monastery. He was identified by the fifth Gyalwa Karmapa, Deshin Shekpa, as the omniscient emanation of the Indian mahāsiddha Tilopa. This was the fulfillment of the prediction made by Tilopa after he received teachings directly from Vajrayoginī in the western land of Uḍḍiyāna. At that time, Tilopa pledged to return to spread these teachings widely after they had been transmitted through thirteen successive lineage holders. Before Tilopa's return this set of teachings was to be limited to a one-to-one transmission from each lineage holder to the next, and only upon Tilopa's later emanation as the first Gharwang Tulku were they opened up to a larger audience. These teachings form the core of the Zurmang Ear-Whispered Lineage.

Recognition

Rinpoche was born a son of the Sikkimese Royal Court. His uncle was then the reigning king of Sikkim. Even before his birth, the sixteenth Gyalwa Karmapa identified him as the twelfth Zurmang Gharwang. His Holiness the Karmapa, who had alluded to his attendants that the next incarnation of Zurmang Gharwang would soon occur, was attending a performance of a traditional Tibetan drama on the forecourt of Rumtek Monastery. During the Tilopa dance, a jewel offering was made to the Karmapa, and breaking with tradition, instead of accepting it himself, the Karmapa directed that the gift be given to the Gharwang Tulku. So saying, he pointed to the surprised mother-to-be and announced that she was carrying the twelfth Gharwang Rinpoche.

A few months later, the Royal Princess delivered her son at her residence in Gangtok. At dawn Rinpoche's parents dispatched a messenger to go to Rumtek, fifteen miles away, to inform His Holiness the Karmapa of the new arrival. However, before the messenger could leave the house, the late Saljay Rinpoche, the Karmapa's emissary, was already at the door with a party of monks, bearing gifts and a letter containing the Karmapa's blessings for the newborn child. Even more bewildering was that at the time when the new tulku was born, the mother of the previous Gharwang, living in Tibet, was heard joyously announcing that "Rinpoche has returned. He is born in a warm country where fruits and flowers grow in abundance, and in the midst of bird song." Her description of the environment surrounding the birth of the new incarnation aptly described Sikkim.

Enthronement

In 1976, shortly after his eleventh birthday, Gharwang Rinpoche was installed on the Lion Throne as the twelfth Zurmang Gharwang. The ceremony took place in the assembly hall of the Dharma Chakra Center in the presence of His Holiness the sixteenth Gyalwa Karmapa. It was well attended by many tulkus, monks, and state dignitaries. Hundreds of well-wishers and devotees came from far and wide to witness the auspicious event.

During the ceremonial installation His Holiness the Karmapa also predicted the founding of a new Zurmang Kagyu monastery outside Tibet, which would become an important center for the teaching and practice of the Buddha Dharma.

Education

In the years following his enthronement, Gharwang Rinpoche received many personal empowerments, textual transmissions, and oral instructions directly from his root lama, the sixteenth Gyalwa Karmapa. After the passing of His Holiness, Gharwang Rinpoche studied at the Nalanda Buddhist Institute between 1981 and 1991, and graduated as the top student in the year of 1991.

Activities

Gharwang Rinpoche began his teaching career at the Nalanda Buddhist Institute. Since then, he has taught extensively in Dharma centers all over the world, in Europe, America, and Asia. Zurmang centers can now be found in Singapore, Hong Kong, Indonesia, and Malaysia.

In August 1991, Gharwang Rinpoche returned for the first time to his original seat in Zurmang, Kham (Qinghai province), amid a rapturous welcome. During this memorable visit, Gharwang Rinpoche gave empowerments to well over thirty thousand people, many of them tulkus and monks, as well as the lay community. Thousands came to take refuge with him, and he bestowed personal blessings upon all those who came to greet him.

In 1992, Gharwang Rinpoche commenced the construction of a new seat for the Zurmang Kagyu Tradition in Lingdum, Sikkim. The site covers approximately twenty-one acres of forested slope on the same hill occupied by Rumtek. In under four years, a magnificent monastic complex was built, fulfilling the sixteenth Gyalwa Karmapa's prediction of a new Zurmang Kagyu monastery outside of Tibet.

Gharwang Rinpoche continues to teach Tibetan Buddhist meditation and philosophy worldwide.

What to Read Next from Wisdom Publications

Mahāmudrā
The Moonlight—Quintessence of Mind and Meditation
Dakpo Tashi Namgyal

"Has helped numerous serious Dharma students."
—His Holiness the Dalai Lama

The Mind of Mahāmudrā
Advice from the Kagyü Masters
Peter Alan Roberts

"Quite simply, the best anthology of Tibetan Mahāmudrā texts yet to appear."
—Roger R. Jackson, Carleton College, author of *Tantric Treasures*

Mahāmudrā and Related Instructions
Core Teachings of the Kagyü Schools
Peter Alan Roberts

"This collection is a treasury of 'great seal' teachings from the most renowned gurus of the Mahāmudrā lineage, each text precious beyond compare. Every page exudes freshness of realization, holding the keys to our own personal awakening."
—Judith Simmer-Brown, Naropa University, author of *Dakini's Warm Breath*

The Karmapas and Their Mahamudra Forefathers
An Illustrated Guide
Khenpo Sherap Phüntsok
Translated by Michele Martin

"This collection of inspiring stories and beautiful artwork presents a glimpse into the lives of some of the greatest masters of the Kagyu lineage. These stories have been passed down from teacher to student for centuries. Filled with profound teachings and practical guidance on the path of awakening, this volume will be of great interest to all those who wish to embody compassion and wisdom."
—Mingyur Rinpoche, author of *The Joy of Living*

Luminous Melodies
Essential Dohās of Indian Mahāmudrā
Karl Brunnhölzl

"These beautiful songs of experience offer glimpses into the awakened minds of the Mahāmudrā masters of India. Karl Brunnhölzl's masterful translations are a joy to read for how they express what is so often inexpressible."
—His Eminence the Twelfth Zurmang Gharwang Rinpoche

Luminous Mind
The Way of the Buddha
Kyabje Kalu Rinpoche

"Undoubtedly the best collection of Kalu Rinpoche's teachings. In perusing these pages, I relived the days when I translated for Rinpoche, enthralled by his magical blend of anecdotes, crystal clear explanations, and profound instruction."
—Ken McLeod, author of *Wake Up to Your Life*

About Wisdom Publications

Wisdom Publications is the leading publisher of classic and contemporary Buddhist books and practical works on mindfulness. To learn more about us or to explore our other books, please visit our website at wisdomexperience.org or contact us at the address below.

Wisdom Publications
199 Elm Street
Somerville, MA 02144 USA

We are a 501(c)(3) organization, and donations in support of our mission are tax deductible.

Wisdom Publications is affiliated with the Foundation for the Preservation of the Mahayana Tradition (FPMT).